THE *Spirituality* OF MUSIC

JOHN BIRD

THE *Spirituality* OF MUSIC

Northstone

Concept: Northstone Team
Editor: Mike Schwartzentruber
Cover and interior design: Susan Neill and Margaret Kyle
Proofreading: Dianne Greenslade
Photo credits: see page 160

Northstone is an imprint of **Wood Lake Publishing, Inc.**
Wood Lake Publishing acknowledges the financial support
of the Government of Canada, through the Book Publishing
Industry Development Program (BPIDP) for its publishing
activities.

SILVER
BNC CERTIFIED | BIBLIOGRAPHIC DATA 2008-09

Library and Archives Canada
Cataloguing in Publication
Bird, John, 1953-
     The spirituality of music / John Bird.
Includes bibliographical references.
ISBN 978-1-896836-88-1
     1. Music – Philosophy and aesthetics.
2. Music – Religious aspects.
3. Music – Psychological aspects. I. Title.
ML3800.B618 2008   781'.1   C2008-903924-6

Published by Northstone
An imprint of Wood Lake Publishing Inc.
9590 Jim Bailey Road, Kelowna, BC V4V 1R2 Canada
www.woodlakebooks.com
250.766.2778

Printing 10 9 8 7 6 5 4 3 2 1
Printed in China

Contents

DEDICATION

For Lorraine.
I realized I'd fallen in love with you when you played Bach's Arioso *for me,*
your tongue poking out of the corner of your mouth.
You have been unfailingly supportive and
enthusiastic throughout this project.
You have been quick with wise advice when sought,
and wisely refrained from offering it unsought.
A more wonderful partner I could neither ask for nor imagine.

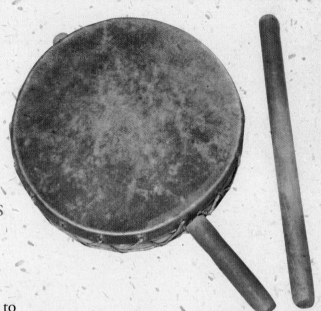

ACKNOWLEDGMENTS

Music is a delightfully convivial pastime and so many people have been part of the musical journey to this book.

First, unstinting thanks to Tony Mason, a great guitar player – and now a good friend – with an encyclopedic knowledge of Americana roots music, for calling together the musicians who became SwingBridge, for welcoming me into the family, and for patiently and enthusiastically teaching me how to contribute with my little ukulele. And to all of SwingBridge for sharing that adventure: Eileen and Robert Blake, Jack Connelly, Bruce Hobley, Ted Laughlin, Allan Reeve, John (J. R.) Robertson, and George Samson.

Thanks also to

— My beloved parents, Peter and Lena Bird, who sang to me, danced with me, and gave me a love and enthusiasm for music and life that has stayed with me always.

— My brother, Jeff Bird, for being my primary musical beacon, and for many late-night hours together listening to and talking about music.

— The (Greater) Peterborough music community, especially Ava Richardson, Myra Hirschberg, Al Kirby, Jim Yates, Peter Wotherspoon, Jay Edmunds and the Kendrick clan, for sharing their musical enthusiasms.

— Iqaluit's Heather Daley, Errol Fletcher, Lorne Levy, and Rob Aubé

If music be the food of love, then play on.

— WILLIAM SHAKESPEARE

for inviting me so graciously into the Road to Nowhere Band.

— Other Iqaluit music makers, especially Darlene Nuqingaq, Mattie McNair, John Laird, John Lamb, Allison Lee, Paula McRae, the Iqaluit Community Choir, and the Aqsarnit Middle School Fiddle Club, for many hours of fun.

— Those who agreed to be interviewed about music and spirituality in their lives as I worked on this book: Madeleine Allakariallak, Njacko Backo, Jeff Bird, Laverne Jacobs, Anguti Johnston, Becky Kilabuk, Matt Nuquingaq, Juan Opitz, Gershon Silins, Sue Smith, and Peter Workman.

— The good people at Wood Lake Publishing, especially editor Mike Schwartzentruber, for saying yes to this book, and for dedicating much time, effort, and resources to bringing the project to fruition.

— My colleague and friend, Donna Sinclair, whose encouragement started me on this course.

— All those folks across time and space whose music or writings about music continue to touch and teach me.

The [scientist] says that the voice comes from the spine, the diaphragm, the abdomen, and the lungs, The mystic says that sound comes from the soul, the heart, and the mind.

— Hazrat Inayat Khan

Wedding Dance

— Anonymous (in the style of Pieter Bruegel the Elder)

1

This Ever-flowing River of Music, Time, and Life

Music accompanies us throughout our lives, from our very first moments to our very last, bringing meaning and heightened emotional awareness to so many of the important occasions and experiences that mark our journey on this earth.

We are conceived in the pulsing rhythms of the sex act, and our life in the womb is nurtured by the comforting throb of our mother's beating heart.

Each year, we mark our birthday with a simple song that renews our sense of personhood and identity within a community of friends and family.

We dance at weddings, to celebrate a friend's or a relative's commitment to enter a new life in holy and sacred partnership with his or her beloved.

We worship the God of our understanding by singing hymns at church, temple, or synagogue.

To stop the flow of music would be like the stopping of time itself, incredible and inconceivable.

– AARON COPLAND

And when our time comes to leave this world, we hope that friends and family will come together to sing us out of it, to celebrate our lives and to wish us godspeed.

But even then, the rhythm and the music will play on.

Nor do we mark just the special moments with music. "The world is inherently musical," says Don Campbell, in his book *The Mozart Effect*. Music's adherents "outnumber the speakers of Mandarin, English, Hindi, Spanish, Russian, and all other tongues combined." Music "rises above all income levels, social classes, educational achievements. Music speaks to everyone – and to every species. Birds make it, snakes are charmed by it, and whales and dolphins serenade one another with it."

Campbell finds strong evidence that before humans learned to speak, we sang – that "music is humanity's original language." He points out, for example, that "researchers have found that about two-thirds of the cilia – the thousands of minute hairs in the inner ear that lie on a flat plane like piano keys and respond to different frequencies of sound – resonate only at the higher, 'musical' frequencies." This would indicate, he says, that for a very long time, "human beings probably communicated primarily with song or tone."

Juan Opitz is a percussionist who came to Toronto as a refugee from his Chilean homeland after the brutal 1973 coup by Augusto Pinochet. "Drums are the most primitive, most basic way of communicating," he told me in an interview. "The most basic, and probably the first. Before language. They created language, starting with drums and sticks."

Soon after arriving in Toronto as a lost and traumatized young man, with many of his friends killed or missing, Opitz helped form Los Compañeros, a fabled band of exiled Chilean and Greek musicians, which Heritage Canada says marked the beginning of the world-beat music movement in this country. For Opitz, drums have played a vital role in his efforts "to find out what I'm doing here, who I am, the eternal questions." And they are his principal way of expressing what he's finding out.

When I hear music I fear no danger, I am invulnerable, I see no foe. I am related to the earliest times and to the latest.

— Henry David Thoreau

EVERYTHING HAS A RHYTHM

So long as the human spirit thrives on this planet, music in some living form will accompany and sustain it and give it expressive meaning.

– AARON COPLAND

So we carry music with us – and it carries us – through our most significant moments as well as through the most mundane activities of our daily lives. We awake to the latest pop or country songs on the clock radio. We sing in the shower. We play CDs in the car during our daily commute, and sport MP3 players while doing aerobics at the gym, or while out running or walking.

We even whistle while we work, whether we're digging a ditch, preparing a report, folding laundry, making dinner, or weeding the garden. As an incidental character in John Sayles' film *Honeydripper* puts it, "Everything in life got a rhythm – even pickin' cotton."

And of course, we use music to help us access our emotional lives, or more precisely, to help us connect our intellect, our so-called rational mind, with our emotions, our bodies, our souls; and to share feelings with one another.

A father's lullaby in the dark of night can send us drifting into "Slumberland," secure in the faith that we are loved, cared for, and protected. I remember my own father lying beside me like a gentle giant in my child's single bed, as I snuggled deeper under the covers, bathed, scrubbed, brushed, combed, and poised on the edge of sleep. His smooth, comforting tenor voice would spin tales for me of cattle drives and of life in the bush, as he gently crooned work songs from his New Brunswick childhood – songs such as the lumber-camp lament *Peter Emberly*; or the cowboy ballads of Wilf Carter, *Streets of Laredo* and *Strawberry Roan*.

My mother shared songs from her Welsh childhood. She would hold me close and sing humorous tunes in a strange, wild language that told me we drew part of our family heritage from a more ancient culture than the popular one I knew through commercial radio. Her songs ran the gamut from Church of Wales hymns such as *Guide Me, O Thou Great Jehovah*, to humorous ditties such as *Sospan Fach* (Little Saucepan) and *Hen Fenyw Fach Cydweli* (The Little Old Lady from Kidwelly).

I also remember my mother and father holding one another tight, drifting across the kitchen floor in a tender, shuffling dance that spoke volumes to my closely watching brother and me about their devotion to one another. They would gaze deeply into each other's eyes, and sing together the romantic pop songs of their Second-World-War youth – songs of hope from amid war and separation: *There'll Be Bluebirds over the White Cliffs of Dover* or *Dream a Little Dream of Me.*

I will always cherish those moments in the kitchen, when music offered me a glimpse into another aspect of my parents' strong and mutual love – and another lesson about the joys of love.

Love doesn't always work out, of course. When it fails, we grieve lost love with a country ballad or heartfelt blues, which can express for us inchoate feelings of heartbreak and loss we might otherwise keep bottled up inside. Even more than that, as we play the songs over and over – and perhaps pour our hearts into singing along – we find a new perspective that assures us that, as George Harrison sang, "all things must pass," including this seemingly endless grief. The music tells us that with a little luck and perseverance, a reciprocal love may yet find its way to our hearts. And when it does, we'll no doubt celebrate that event with other, happier songs. "If music be the food of love," said Shakespeare in Twelfth Night, "play on."

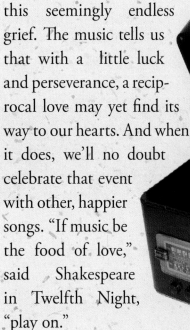

Music Is a Magical Medium

Of course life is not a solo performance and love is more than a duet. And so we turn to the communal experience of music to lift us above our quotidian and sometimes too-small existence. We attend concerts, seeking – hoping for – a few heightened moments when the music will knead us with a thousand other concertgoers into one mystical and rhythmically unified organism. Whether we prefer the sublime sweep of a symphonic orchestra, the soaring voices of a massed choir, or the thundering rhythms of a full-bore rock-and-roll band, one way or another we're pursuing the mystical joy of knowing we're alive, and feeling ourselves collective members of a divine creation.

Perhaps in political struggle – on a picket line or in a march against poverty – we find mutual strength in linking arms and in singing a labour anthem such as *Bread and Roses*, or a protest song such as *We Shall Overcome*, itself a beautiful African-American spiritual that once helped a people persist against the physical and spiritual brutality of slavery.

Then there are the moments of pure, untrammelled animal vitality, when we simply delight in moving our bodies with others to the underlying pulse of life as expressed in an up-tempo disco or soca hit, the hypnotic rhythms of industrial trance music, or the skirling wail of an old-time Cajun or Celtic fiddle tune.

"Music is a magical medium," says Don Campbell, "that moves, enchants, energizes and heals us." It uplifts our souls. People today "spend more money, time and energy on music than on books, movies and sports."

Even at its most physical, though, music continues to remind us of the spiritual connections that reach beyond our corporeal boundaries. It reminds us that we are not autonomous, alienated beings, but integral members of an infinitely larger and more wondrous universe.

And even the seemingly satanic imagery of some heavy-metal head-banger music, or the angry misogyny of certain rappers, while it may be offensive to many of us, can actually empower others who sorely need to understand themselves as something other than helpless and victimized. The rest of us should perhaps hear in such music an angry outcry against a system that continues to divide and discriminate by race, class, or gender.

As for which music is superior to another, comparisons are surely odious. Taste is a matter of personal and cultural history, and it continues to evolve for each of us, and for society, with passing time. Mozart may reach sublime heights that few can match, but I'll still take my mother rocking me in her arms and crooning *I'll Be with You in Apple Blossom Time.*

Jazz Duet
– Ellen Dreibelbis

The principles of music are also principles for good living, expansive, generous and harmony-seeking.

–Sheeba (formerly Jane Siberry)

17

Music is a vehicle for spiritual travel. For thousands and thousands of years – somewhere back there in all of our histories – shamans have ridden the rhythms of the drum into the spirit world, to encounter and enlist the help of animal spirit guides, to wrestle with their own demons, with other people's demons, or with society's demons, and ultimately, to find healing.

And who among us has never felt that sense of being spiritually transported by music, whether by the driving rhythms of a hard-rocking blues band, the smooth sensual throb of a Motown backbeat, or the pure rueful lament of an operatic soprano sighing over a lost love?

Sometimes our intention is more overtly spiritual. We seek to heighten our connection with the God of our understanding by singing together at church, temple, or synagogue; or by attending a performance of Bach's *St. Matthew's Passion* or Handel's *Messiah*.

Members of the Mevlevi Order of Sufi dervishes, in Turkey, per-

God's greatest creation is music. Better than land, wisdom, or being father of 1,000 sons. Music contains all of life.

– INDIAN MUSICIAN IN THE FILM, *GYPSY CARAVAN*

form a spinning dance to the music of strings, flutes, drums, and vocal chanting, seeking spiritual ecstasy. It's their path to God.

Music's spiritual power starts in the preconscious, aqueous comfort of the womb. There, in dim light filtered through flesh, blood, and amniotic fluid, perhaps only barely discerned by still-developing eyes, the pulsing, repetitive thud of our mother's heart, the whoosh of blood through her veins and arteries, the muffled rumble of her voice, and the intermittent gurglings of the digestive system, form the beginnings of a fundamental soundtrack for life.

In Iqaluit, in the Canadian Arctic, where I'm living these days, I've fallen in love with Inuit throat singing. In this wonderfully compelling tradition, two women (it's generally women) will stand face to face in a loose embrace and blend sequences of rhythmic guttural sounds generated in various body cavities, including the depths of the chest or belly,

the throat and mouth, and the nasal and sinus passages. It's often nearly impossible to tell which singer is producing which sounds, as they conjoin to create fascinating polyrhythms and complex combinations of drones, animal-like woofs and grunts, and hypnotic overtones. It's incredibly sophisticated music, and like nothing I've ever heard in my own Western tradition.

Becky Kilabuk, an Inuk throat singer from Iqaluit believes this favourite musical tradition of hers has its origin in the attempts of Inuit mothers to soothe their crying babies. "We wear amauties," she explains, referring to the traditional women's parkas, with the enlarged hood designed to accommodate an infant inside it. "You have the baby right up against your back in the amauti, and often it's bare skin to bare skin. When you make those sounds, you have the vibrations going right down your back. It's soothing to the baby."

Throat singers sound like they have a string in their body. And they sound like they have found a way to bow that string. It seems so earthy, so much a part of nature.

– David Harrington,
violinist, Kronos Quartet

Her theory fits surprisingly well with what French physician Alfred Tomatis describes in his book *The Conscious Ear*: "The universe of sound in which the embryo is submerged is remarkably rich in sound qualities of every kind…internal rumblings, the movement of chyle at the time of digestion, and cardiac rhythms at a sort of gallop."

Tomatis compares it to an African bush at twilight, with "distant calls, echoes, stealthy rustlings, and the lapping of waves," all of which comes remarkably close to describing the qualities of Inuit throat singing, an artistic re-creation of those original sounds in whose embrace we first swam into being. Tomatis concludes that "the embryo draws a feeling of security from this permanent dialogue which guarantees it will have a harmonious blossoming."

That's how primal music can be in our lives.

The discovery of song and the creation of musical instruments both owed their origin to a human impulse which lies much deeper than conscious intention: the need for rhythm in life. The need is a deep one, transcending thought, and disregarded at our peril..

– RICHARD BAKER

21

Music is love in search of a word.

— Sidney Lanier

The first rhythmic body movement we make of our own volition, suggests Grateful Dead percussionist Mickey Hart in his fascinating book *Drumming at the Edge of Magic*, is the instinctual sucking movement of the newborn infant at the breast. It's a rhythm that brings us sustenance, offers comfort, and ensures survival.

And it reconnects us to our mothers, that wonderful, all-powerful creature whose genetic material we share, and who carried and sheltered us within her own flesh during those long nine months of unborn life. Her rhythmically pulsing heart stood in for our own, still-developing heart. It fed and sustained us without cease, bringing life-giving nourishment, oxygen and warmth, until eventually the rhythmic contractions of the womb and birth canal propelled us into the open air of a brave new world, and we began to take over these life-sustaining rhythms for ourselves. Our lungs began expanding and contracting, our hearts pumped blood, our mouths sucked milk — and so, in rhythms, we began the process of becoming unique human beings, of separating from our mothers.

Such rhythmical pulsations may predate conscious memory, but we all carry some variation on these experiences as part of our body memories.

Small wonder, then, that rhythm is basic to our sense of self, including our sense of ourselves as spiritual beings in this world. Rhythm carries us beyond our egos and connects us to other people, to the natural creation, and to what Paul Tillich called our "Ground of Being" — the ultimate, moving life force to which we all owe our existence and which many of us call God.

Rhythm is the foundation of all music, even more fundamental than melody or harmony. You can't play two notes in succession without the

Seemed to me that drumming was the best way to get close to God.

– Lionel Hampton

beginnings of rhythm. As Mickey Hart says in his book, "Strike a membrane with a stick, the ear fills with noise – unmelodious, inharmonic sound. Strike it a second time, a third, you've got rhythm." But not yet melody, since we don't perceive pitch in many percussion instruments.

"Rhythms are of sufficient interest to us," he adds, "that information about them is routed to a whole other part of the brain than information about tone or melody or meaning. Rhythm [by which he means pattern] is one of the things we are coded to scan for." You can't

Bach Fugue

— Kristin Morris

have rhythm without repetition, and "once you've observed enough repetitions you can say there's a pattern."

It is from patterns that we make meaning. And meaning – along with connection, for the two go hand in hand – is the essence of our lifelong spiritual quest. What is life without meaning, and meaning without connection? As the Greek philosopher Socrates so succinctly put it several thousand years ago, "The unexamined life is not worth living."

So begins our journey in music, and so begins the musical journey of this book. Someone once said that "writing about music is like dancing about architecture – it's a really stupid thing to want to do." It's such a great quote that (as Allan P. Scott documents extensively on his webpage) it has been variously attributed to as diverse a cast of characters as Elvis Costello, Martin Mull, Clara Schumann, Igor Stravinsky, David Byrne, Frank Lloyd Wright, Thelonious Monk, Frank Zappa, Laurie Anderson, Steve Martin, William S. Burroughs, Charles Mingus, Nick Lowe, Miles Davis, George Carlin and/or John Cage. Take your pick.

Without music, life is a journey through a desert.

— PAT CONROY

Regardless of who said it first, it's a great statement because it gets to the heart of the matter: music is meant to be experienced directly. Music deals with meanings and emotions that often can't be put into words.

Aaron Copland, one of my favourite American composers, reportedly expressed it another way:

The whole problem can be stated quite simply by asking, "Is there a meaning to music?" My answer would be, "Yes." And "Can you state in so many words what the meaning is?" My answer to that would be, "No."

Copland also said, "If a literary man puts together two words about music, one of them will be wrong."

Nevertheless, when we're not experiencing music – and even while we are – we continue to talk about it. And I'm going to continue to try to write about it. Because it's important. And because, in case it's not obvious already, I love music. I love to listen to it, to watch people play it. I love to dance to it, meditate to it, and particularly I love to play it myself – and especially to play it with other people.

"Everybody has a heart," Juan Opitz told me.

To follow your heart – literally – just put your hand on your heart and repeat its rhythm with your other hand with a drum or a stick. That's you. That's your rhythm. Your rhythm is not in your face, your body, your physical appearance. The colour of your skin can be totally different than mine. Your heart is the same. It's only one beat, and that's the human beat – and if you want to go farther, the universal beat.

Welcome to the universal beat of music.

Jondo 1
— Alex Mackenzie

*Music is spiritual.
The music business
is not.*
— Van Morrison

*His sound was stunning
– it was the blues, it was
R&B, it was gospel, it
was swing – it was all
the stuff I was listening
to before that but rolled
into one amazing,
soulful thing.*

— Van Morrison

29

Music Warp
— Jerry Clovis

2

A Consuming Passion

Engaging Music as an Avid Listener

I'm growing older (aren't we all). I'm beginning to feel the weight of the years. There are times I can be quite curmudgeonly, especially when it comes to crowds. I avoid them.

But there was a moment, half a lifetime ago, when I was young and enthusiastic, and prone to fits of ecstasy – much like my son Tom is now, in his early 20s.

Sometimes I like to recall those days. Sometimes I even attempt to revisit them.

So here we are, Tom and I, shuffling along in a massive lineup with 35,000 other Van Morrison fans, trying to get into a wet field on the edge of downtown Ottawa to hear the venerable Irish soul singer open the Ottawa Blues Festival.

Perhaps not surprisingly, I'm feeling rather grumpy. It took me four hours to drive here. I'll sleep

The child who is raised with an ear pure and clear may not be able to play the popular tunes on the violin or the piano, but I do not think this has anything to do with the ability to hear true music or to sing. It is when the heart is filled with song that the child can be said to be musically gifted.

– Masanobu Fukuoka

on the floor of a friend's TV room tonight, and spend another four hours driving home tomorrow.

I paid a small fortune for our tickets, and I'm already feeling crowded and uncomfortable. Inside it'll be worse. We'll never get to use our folding chairs; we'll have to stand for the whole show. We'll be miles from the stage.

To quote Winnie the Pooh's despondent pal Eeyore, "It'll probably rain."

I'm right about it all, unfortunately (except, thank goodness, the rain). Inside, we try to work our way forward. But the crowd jams up tighter and tighter until we give up, still the better part of a football field away from the stage, where the roadies look like ants.

I try to put on a happy face for Tom, but inside I'm harrumphing like a superannuated steam locomotive.

Right on time (thank God for small mercies), a perky young DJ comes out to pump up the crowd.

As she finishes, the band kicks in, and suddenly there's Van himself, striding onstage and launching into *Talk Is Cheap*. Good news: the man is here to sing, not talk. But then that's always been his way.

We can barely see him up on the stage, but a large, high-definition screen looms nearby, offering a 20-foot-tall image of Van's sharp-nosed phizog under a white, straw, Panama hat. Who could mistake that voice, those growls, that phrasing, that Belfast twang, as he leans back, eyes closed, and sinks into the music?

The crowd roars its approval. Tom is ecstatic.

For the next hour and a half, Van keeps the show rolling from song to song, delivering a virtual "best of" set in reverse. It spans about 40 years, starting with some of his most recent songs, such as *All Work, No Play*, moving backwards through *Cleaning Windows* and the venerable *Moondance*, to his first and biggest chart topper, *Brown-*

Eyed Girl, before ending with a driving piece of blues-rock he wrote and sang while still a teenager with a band called Them.

In his book *Runaway American Dream,* Jimmy Guterman calls Morrison's music "strange and wondrous." It's "Celtic rhythm-and-blues with horns that could blow down the walls of a city," he says, "and words that either expressed profound thoughts or melted into roaring and scatting as Morrison hunted for a place beyond words, a peaceful home safe from the tyranny of language. He never did find it for long, but that didn't stop his bloodhound search."

Despite my best efforts, I only manage to remain miserable till about halfway through Van's second song. The sound is great, with instruments and voices all clear and well-balanced. The video screen is picture perfect. The songs are little masterpieces. By the end of his set, I'm pumping my fist in the air along with all the beautiful, sensitive people around me, and shouting along with them the chorus to Van's first hit, "G-L-O-R-I-A, Gloooria."

You can't stay the same. If you're a musician and a singer, you have to change, that's the way it works.

– VAN MORRISON

If a man does not keep pace with his companions, perhaps it is because he hears a different drummer. Let him step to the music which he hears, however measured or far away.

– Henry David Thoreau

I went into this concert feeling like Oscar the Grouch. But I came out loving the world, and everyone around me; people who, like Tom and me, have weaknesses, fears, and anxieties about life. I'm filled with joy just to be alive, and to be here with my son. I still recognize that pain, loss, and transience are integral to the human condition, but I understand, too, that they're what give life its joyous sense of connection, its poignancy, and its beauty.

Music writer Clive Culbertson describes Van Morrison's genius as his ability, when he's on form, to "allow the presence to come in him." He's got soul, and in this 90-minute set the music of his soul has touched ours – and encouraged our souls to touch one another.

Being able to feel something is "the greatest freedom in the world," said Memphis recording genius Sam Phillips, who helped bring people like Elvis Presley, Johnny Cash, Howlin' Wolf and Carl Perkins to the world. Phillips told writer Jimmy Guterman, "That's what I wanted my records to make you do. That's all. That's it." At its most elemental, he explained, music is "just a man beating on the side of a wooden box." But, "there's nothing like it: No painting, no sermon, no book, nothing."

Thank you, Van Morrison. That's what you delivered tonight in spades.

And if that's not spiritual, I want to know what is?

As listeners, we typically go to a concert seeking what screenplay writer and teacher Robert McKee calls a "meaningful emotional experience." His reference is to film, but the description applies to all art. In the case of music, the performer can't give us that "meaningful emotional experience" unless we're willing to participate too. Every live concert situation, every audience, has a vibe, which the performers can manipulate and help amplify to a degree. But they can't control it without the listeners' collusion. The musicians might have hold of the reins, but they can still be bucked off. In many ways, they're just along for the ride too. "In the East, 'Original Mind' signifies observing the world fresh, with the purity and innocence of a child," says Don Campbell in *The Mozart Effect*. "The first step in listening well is to listen with childlike wonder." As Gandhi, one of history's most patient listeners, reminds us, "If we have listening ears, God speaks to us in our own language, whatever that language is.'"

My younger brother, Jeff Bird, a professional musician with four decades of experience, says that in a performance situation, the interaction between musicians and audience is an essential part of how it all works – or doesn't. "It's a two-way street."

Chilean-born percussionist Juan Opitz first began to grasp this dynamic while playing

*Music is the art of
thinking with sounds.*

– JULES COMBARIEU

at a coffeehouse in Toronto soon after he arrived there as a political refugee in the mid 1980s. "That's what we realized at the Trojan Horse [coffee house]," he told me in an interview. "We were in very close proximity with the audience. We could see their every reaction. We could feel the vibration, what they were thinking, what they were feeling at that moment. Because we were just a metre away. We were one big body, one big soul, one big spirit there. And we established that connection."

Sometimes, he adds, it's the silences in the music – "the space, the dynamics" – that allow for the best listener engagement. "The silence is sometimes the place where the message results. Because the message is not what I give you. It's the message you receive, as an audience."

MUSIC AS THE MEANS OF SALVATION

Beginning in the 1970s, and right through to today, New Jersey native Bruce Springsteen has continued to win hearts and souls with his powerful songs, which meld rhythm and blues roots with rockabilly to tell tales of passionate yearning. Underlying it all is his obvious sincerity and powerful faith that the music, if it only be pure enough, can be the means of salvation from all that human angst and yearning. Bruce is a true believer in the redemptive power of rock and roll, and he found a world of true believers waiting for him in what many would describe as a soulless suburban wasteland. Springsteen celebrates a "world in which artists can find fountains in deserts," says Guterman. It's a "world in which nothing can hold back the power of music to change everything about you."

One summer when I was in my early 30s, Springsteen came to town to play two concerts at Toronto's now-demolished Exhibition Stadium. I resisted the temptation to attend the first night (too expensive, too busy), but after hearing the rave

reviews in the media the next day, I made a last minute attempt to get into the second show.

I was too late, as it turned out. By the time I got there, the tickets were sold out and even the scalpers had gone home. But it was a warm, summer evening, and as the concert started I found I could hear the music fairly well from outside the stadium. I wandered around until I found myself at a back corner with a couple dozen other fans who had lined themselves up so they could see through a gap at a gate and catch the occasional glimpse of Bruce projected onto one of the stadium screens. I stayed there for about an hour, marvelling at the warm and wonderful sense of camaraderie among these fellow outcasts, who seemed to know all the words to Springsteen's songs. And they all sang along. It was an experience whose power lay in the sense of connection these fans found in their shared love of Bruce's music.

"It may be," says Don Campbell, "that Bruce Springsteen is a contemporary working man's Orpheus, embodying the plight of modern youth in the act of slogging its way through the Underworld, in search of some lost beloved and making countless mistakes and wrong turns." It's an image of the singer as "urban shaman."

A Disembodied Voice across Starry Skies

Most of us, myself included, spend our lives as a consumers of other people's music. The development and explosion in recording and playback technology is the big story in music history over the last century, a hallmark of the electronic age. Starting with Edison's gramophone and the development of wax cylinders, and moving through 78-rpm discs, long-playing records, cassette and 8-track tapes, compact discs, and now MP3 players – not to mention radio – consuming music has become a fingertip exercise.

It's been a century since we've had to make music ourselves, if we were in the mood to hear some. Or since we've had to have someone make it in front of us.

Many of us still have boxes of LPs (or perhaps they're in milk crates, which miraculously were the perfect size for those old records) mouldering away in our attic or basement. And whole industries have grown up to provide shelving for, first, cassette tapes, and then CDs. Nowadays many of us listen to music on our computers. In fact, I'm listening right now, as I write this, through headphones so as not to disturb my wife.

> *Music is everybody's possession. It's only publishers who think that people own it.*
>
> – John Lennon

Feeling Blue

- TODD HORNE

These developments have opened up huge worlds of music to our thirsty ears, minds, and hearts. They've brought the soul of other peoples and traditions right into our living rooms, and have even contributed to diminishing racial prejudice, as we've learned to appreciate one another's musical cultures.

Radio, too, has had an immeasurable impact on our listening patterns and on our musical educations. Most of us, as teenagers, had that strange, delicious experience of lying in bed at night, discovering a wider world through a disembodied voice and strange new combinations of rhythmic and melodic sounds beamed across dark, starry skies and into our ears.

No wonder radio has a reputation as being the most intimate of the media.

The baby-boom bulge came of age just in time to embrace, first, the folk boom of the early 1960s, and then the "British Invasion," led by the Beatles, who revolutionized the popular music of North America. It is sadly ironic that British bands like the Rolling Stones, the Spencer Davis Group, and Eric Burdon and The Animals crossed the North American racial divide and introduced white America (and Canada) to the Mississippi Delta blues of acoustic Afro-American performers such as Robert Johnson, Charlie Patton, and Son House; and to urban, electrified performers out of Chicago and Memphis (although with roots in the same Delta cotton plantations) such as Muddy Waters, Howlin' Wolf, B. B. King, and T-Bone Walker.

It grew even more exciting to many white teens when some of those British bands – the Stones, Cream, Led Zeppelin – took the seminal country blues of people like Robert Johnson, and cranked it up with overdriven electric guitars and booming drums and bass. Perfect for adolescence.

Are we not formed, as notes of music are, For one another, though dissimilar?

– Percy Bysshe Shelley

You know, music, it's spiritual. You can take a small kid, that can't even sit alone, and you pull the strings on some kind of instrument, a fiddle or a banjo or something like that, and you watch how quickly it draws the attention of that kid. And he'll do his best to get a hold of that. It draws the attention of the whole human race.

— ROSCOE HOLDOM

"Anyone who's grown up a rock-and-roll fan," says Guterman, "connects art with yearning, be it romantic, spiritual, political, economic, or otherwise. Rock and roll is not music about being satisfied; it's music about shouting that you 'can't get no satisfaction.'"

That's not just true of rock and roll, mind you. It's a condition common to much popular music down through the ages. Consider the lyrics from *Plaisir d'Amour,* a French chanson that's over 200 years old: "Plaisir d'amour dura qu'un instant. Chagrin d'amour dure toute la vie." ("The pleasure of love lasts but an instant. The sorrow of love lasts a whole life long.") Or the old English song *Greensleeves,* sometimes attributed to Henry VIII: "Alas my love, you do me wrong, to cast me off discourteously." There you have the templates for 90 percent of pop music through the ages.

Because, of course, whether it's the 1540s, the 1780s, the 1940s, or right through to today, the popular music business all over the world is tailored to appeal to teens and young adults, by engaging them over their primary, hormone-driven preoccupations: love, mating, and meaning. Adolescence brings new, exciting, powerful, and scary feelings and emotions to the surface. What better way to explore them, process them, and discover you are not alone in going through them, than with music, the emotional art?

"Music expresses that which cannot be put into words and that which cannot remain silent," said the French writer Victor Hugo. Blues singer B. B. King said, "singing about your sadness unburdens your soul." Composer Noel Coward, very popular in his day, expressed it a little more cynically, although I suspect that deep down he was not being cynical at all, when he said, "it's extraordinary how potent cheap music is."

Untitled

— Jim Kalin

Joy, sorrow, tears, lamentation, laughter – to all these music gives voice, but in such a way that we are transported from the world of unrest to a world of peace, and see reality in a new way, as if we were sitting by a mountain lake and contemplating hills and woods and clouds in the tranquil and fathomless water.

— Albert Schweitzer

How many of us, as teens, have spent countless hours alone in our rooms, or perhaps with a best friend as confidant, mooning over a beautiful young woman or man who, for reasons then unfathomable, wouldn't give us the time of day. We wallowed in the sentiment of "cheap music" – Janis Joplin singing, "take another little piece of my heart"; the Temptations admitting that their idealized relationship was "just my imagination, running away with me"; Bob Marley crooning, "I don't want to wait in vain for your love"; or Dion and the Belmonts warning us to "stay away from run-around Sue."

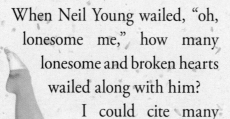

When Neil Young wailed, "oh, lonesome me," how many lonesome and broken hearts wailed along with him?

I could cite many thousands of songs of that nature, and for each of them there will be someone among us, or more likely, many some-ones, who benefited from their guidance, from the pure entertainment they offered us, but most of all, from their simple yet profound ability to express that which could not remain silent. Music's power, says Oliver Wendell Holmes, "dwells not in the tones but in the echoes of our hearts."

We all know, however, that the music of youth, while containing more than its share of emotional love songs, is not limited to those genres. Don Campbell writes that the growing body – and I would add, the growing soul – "needs to drum and move, sing and dance, release pressure, and find its own natural rhythm. Modern society doesn't always allow for this, however, and so a potent form of music has arisen to fill the void."

Teens and young adults are generally bubbling over with youthful vigour, and coming into the peak of their physical and sexual powers (if not necessarily sophistication). They have energy to burn, and burning it ofttimes gets them into trouble. Much better to burn through music and dance. When John Lee Hooker said he wanted to "boogie, till the break of dawn," thousands of teens and young adults responded at once with heart and soul: "Me too!" Alice Cooper screamed, "I'm 18; I don't know what I want," to a generation of youth turning something like 18 themselves and filled with vaguely understood, hormone-driven wants. Lou Reed sang, "take a walk on the wild side," and most of his generation soon realized it would be much smarter and healthier to let Lou take that walk and to follow along vicariously, courtesy of his music.

But among all the different arts, the art of music has been especially considered divine, because it is the exact miniature of the law working through the whole universe.

– Hazrat Inayat Khan

And for those who did walk a little too far down that road, there was always the promise of comfort and redemption to be found in Rod Stewart's surprisingly fervent rendition of the classic hymn *Amazing Grace,* or in George Harrison's deeply spiritual album, *All Things Must Pass.*

Speaking for myself, it wasn't just pop and folk music that resonated in my heart, even as a teen. I spent many hours on the living room floor in front of my parents' stereo absorbing the recordings my mother had bought as part of a series of "great classics" distributed through the local grocery store. I used to lose myself in – and never failed to feel my soul stirred by – the surging strings and tripping clarinet, oboe, and flute in Beethoven's Sixth Symphony, the *Pastorale.* I fell deeply in love with the sweetly soaring solo violin in Vaughan Williams' *The Lark Ascending.* Listening to that was almost an out-of-body experience; very meditative.

And then there was the hymnody of the Anglican Church and the English choral tradition, with which I grew up – choral works by composers like Tallis, Byrd, and Canada's own Healey Willan, as interpreted by the choir of Kings College, Cambridge (England), or some of the great cathedral choirs of England and Canada. Those choral introductions also brought me to the Gregorian chant of the monks of the Benedictine Abbey at Solesmes, France, whose sonorous melodies reflected the deep peace of a life devoted to God.

It's all grist for the mill of the soul.

Music washes away from the soul the dust of everyday life.

– BERTHOLD AUERBACH

45

It's Sexual...and It's Holy

Back in the late 1960s and early 1970s, the Mariposa Folk Festival was held on Toronto's Ward Island, one of a crescent of tree-dappled, beach-ringed islets that protect the city's harbour from the storms of Lake Ontario, and that form the jewel in the crown of its parks system. You reach the Toronto Islands by ferry boat, and the ride offers a magical view of the city across the harbour, especially at dusk on a lush midsummer evening, as the last daylight fades over the water, the evening star and a crescent moon gradually coalesce out of the darkening sky, and the lights of the down-town towers glow brighter against a sky turning cobalt blue.

One magical festival day ended in an intimate, firefly-lit glade with a concert by legendary bluesman Taj Mahal. As the last daylight was fading, Taj bounded onto the small stage, alone and supported only by a miniscule sound system with a couple of microphones, and no special lighting. Standing well over six feet tall in jeans, denim shirt, leather vest, and wide-brimmed hat, he was the picture of youthful Afro-American vitality, health, and bodily vigour. Everyone was in love with him, men as well as women.

Taj raised a conch shell to his lips and blew two long trumpeting blasts that immediately brought the crowd to its feet as one, roaring back in delighted affirmation of the conch's clarion call. Then, accompanied only by an infectious percussive rhythm he clapped out with his hands – alternately beating them against his chest, abdomen, thighs or one another – Taj launched into a gospel-inspired chant:

Rise up children, shake the devil out your body.

Rise up children, shake the devil out your soul.

Shake the devil out your body. O-o-oh yeah.

Shake the devil out your soul.

Shake the devil out your body. O-o-oh yeah.

Shake the devil out your soul.

The message was clear and absolutely joyous as he repeated the chant over and over, improvising syncopated variations that soon had the crowd sweat-soaked and gasping for breath as they jumped and whirled in place in an ecstatic dance, and echoed back his lines in a traditional call-and-response. It conjured up images of a rural black Southern Baptist church service, a work gang laying railway track, or to go back to the real source, a West African village celebration. Taj was telling us in the clearest, most fun way possible, through his music, "You've got a body. Don't be ashamed of it. Use it. Celebrate it. It's not of the devil; it's sexual and it's holy." And that was welcome news indeed.

It was like another occasion that writer Stephen Foehr would later describe in the book *Taj Mahal: Autobiography of a Bluesman*, which Foehr co-wrote with Taj: "Now, bent over his guitar, he calls out, 'Sock it to me, sock it to me,' and then utters such sounds that it's unclear, lyrically, if they are words at all." Rather, says Foehr, it's like some out-of-the-mind energy responding to the blasting, white-hot band, the music rocketing away from words and into spontaneous emotion. The audience is jumping up and down, leaping into the music that they sense can spin out of control. They want to go out of control with it, to be taken out of themselves. That's why they've come to the concert.

I don't let my mouth say nothin' my head can't stand.

– Louis 'Satchmo' Armstrong

47

Indeed, isn't that why we all listen to music or go to concerts? We want to be taken out of ourselves. And on that evening, Taj – and the music – delivered. Better than drugs.

"Some performers have additional energy flowing in when they perform," says spiritual writer Eckhart Tolle. "There's enormous enthusiasm which everybody can feel and they almost want to soak it up."

I have more than a dozen of Taj's nearly 50 albums and I know I'll get more. His music is always funky and physical, quirky and soulful. It unearths different traditions, creates new traditions, and above all, celebrates a joy in living that grounds me to the earth and connects me with the rest of humanity, and indeed, with the rest of creation. That's what all good music does for me, for my spirit.

Music is a powerful instrument that can connect us with all that is greater than ourselves, with our fellow human beings, and with the greater sea of humanity; what the church calls the communion of saints. It can also connect us with nature, with Mother Earth. And, of course, with what theologian Paul Tillich called our "ground of being," our Creator, our God, however and whatever we imagine God or that creative energy to be.

"Music," says Taj Mahal in his autobiography, "is a major energy from the universe that is stepped down through human consciousness. It's a bigger thing than most people are aware. We're working in a world that tends to try to control nature and surround it in some kind of way. What I'm saying is that the style of the West is to put a corral around lightning. You cannot stop lightning from its own will."

"With the blues I'm really not singing the past," he adds. "I bring the past with the present and then step on out of line to go further. And when an artist goes further out than most people, then it's their responsibility to bring the information back and articulate it in such a way people can understand."

Jeff Bird has a similar take on it. "Good players – like Glenn Gould – it's like they're showing you that clarity, through the clarity of their performance. It's like a little window into that other world, the spiritual world. I think that's part of your job as a performer. It's to show people that window into how the universe works."

Jeff was a founding and long-time member of Tamarack, one of Canada's seminal traditional music bands and, more recently, for many years has helped anchor the musical foundations of the internationally respected Canadian alt-pop group the Cowboy Junkies. A multi-instrumentalist, he has specialized over the years in mandolin, harmonica, and bass, and can still play a mean fiddle too. (Back when we were kids, Jeff picked up my violin after I had already been labouring over it for a year-and-a-half, and within weeks had left me in his rosin dust.)

While still a teenager, Jeff began playing with a friend named Gus Dekking, a singer-guitarist. One night, I heard them perform in a small pub in downtown Oshawa, Ontario. When Jeff took the lead on a medley of traditional fiddle tunes, there was a fiery passion in his playing that gave me goosebumps and took my breath away. This is blood of my blood, and flesh of my flesh, I thought. I had a mystical sense that I was hearing something out of a dimly understood, collective Celtic past we shared, and that he had somehow managed to conjure this from deep within himself – or perhaps from beyond himself. For me, a window opened into my soul, and music is what made it happen.

There can be little doubt (to paint with a broad brush for a moment) that the music industry – the people who get most artists to the recording studios, and who manufacture, market, and distribute the music, for a price, to our eagerly awaiting hands and ears – there can be little doubt that these people are not always the friends of artistic integrity and of the soul of the music. Not that they are against such qualities in principle, but rather that for them these qualities are found far down the ladder in a hierarchy of needs that puts the highest possible profit for the corporate owners at the top.

This is bound to have a negative effect on musical artists, as well as on us, the music lovers, who find ourselves pushed hither and yon by the music companies' marketing departments. Not only do they limit what is available to us, they work hard at moulding our minds – especially the minds of those among us who are young and most vulnerable – to accept what they have to offer.

"You will be excused if you read the words 'hip-hop' and think 'multibillion dollar business that glorifies gangster culture, homophobia and misogyny,'" writes Kevin Spurgaitis in *The United Church Observer*. "But it wasn't always thus." In the early days, "and in the hands of seminal groups such as the Last Poets and Public Enemy, it emphasized social consciousness instead of conspicuous consumption." Says Spurgaitis, "gangsterism is a moneymaker for record companies – 'black manhood in a bottle.'" The result is that Public Enemy, although still performing, has been without a major-label record contract for eight years. Band frontperson, Chuck D, says Spurgaitis, "argues that the record companies coax African Americans to perform

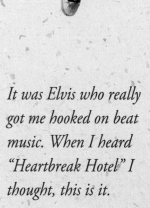

It was Elvis who really got me hooked on beat music. When I heard "Heartbreak Hotel" I thought, this is it.

– PAUL MCCARTNEY

in metaphorical blackface, to shuck and jive for a majority white audience… Commercial hip-hop, as a result, is as put-on as black-dye baseball caps and do-rags."

Horror stories abound in all types of pop music. Look what the industry did to poor child prodigy Brittany Spears: dressed her like a hooker and marketed her as a sex symbol from an unconscionably early age, and helped drive her into mental illness – with complete media collusion, of course, but that's all part of the same system, often with cross ownership.

Then there's the story of Canadian rock icon Neil Young, who was once sued by his record company, Geffen, after he took a new artistic turn and delivered a recording the company deemed "unrepresentative music," meaning it did not sound enough like what they expected from him.

"What I saw for myself," says Taj Mahal in his autobiography, "was that this huge music business is really going to blot out people even thinking about playing music for the soul and heart of themselves, humanity, culture, or anything like that."

So my advice is to forget about the big-business side of music and to investigate the obscure tributaries – whatever truly catches your fancy and isn't just the result of someone's slick marketing efforts. Don't let anyone tell you what you "should" be listening to. Yes, there are some marvels out there getting big media exposure – I've mentioned Van Morrison and Bruce Springsteen among others, and I've enjoyed my concert experiences of people like them. But I'd much prefer to catch a competent small-town band playing for the love of the music in an intimate and affordable venue. Go to small clubs, dances, and coffeehouses. Become an expert in your own musical corner, a student of music history. Use the Internet to follow up whatever catches your fancy. It's a fabulous research tool with great sites such as myspace.com and YouTube, where you can find people who are making some fascinating music in relative obscurity.

If you go to YouTube looking for music-related clips, I guarantee you won't be disappointed. You can watch videos of performances by virtually every musician (including my brother) that I have listed in this book, provided, of course, that they lived during the time of film and sound recording. Just type a name into the YouTube search engine and see what comes up. You can also search by your favourite instrument or genre of music. The results will amaze you. In February 2008, I did a search for "harmonica" and got 28,100 hits; a search for "jazz" produced 335,000 hits. This means that there are that many video clips available that are, in one way or another, related to the harmonica and to jazz, respectively. (Since more videos are being added all the time, the results will, of course, be quite different by the time you read this.)

The most exciting thing about the Internet, musically speaking, and particularly at this point about YouTube, is that it is putting music making and music sharing back into the hands of amateurs, the true music lovers.

If ya ain't got it in ya, ya can't blow it out.
– LOUIS 'SATCHMO' ARMSTRONG

Gershon Silins, a professional cantor at Toronto's Temple Sinai, recalled for me the experience of listening to Leon Fleisher's recent recording of Schubert's piano sonata in B-flat major. "Fleisher lost the use of his right hand decades ago," Silins told me. "And he encountered a treatment that brought back his ability to play with both hands only a few years ago. So he started to record again, and it's a miraculous rebirth. You can hear that miracle in his playing. That Schubert sonata is one of the moments that I find most compelling. He doesn't have great chops anymore as a pianist, but he's a great soul as a musician."

As famed concert violinist Itzhak Perlman has put it, "Sometimes it is the artist's task to find out how much music you can still make with what you have left." Perhaps the real miracle in this case is that Fleisher's loss of the use of his right hand freed him from the world of the professional concert musician so that, when he eventually regained its use, he found

himself once again with the wonder of beginner's mind, the soul of the amateur, which means "lover of."

"When you do things from your soul you feel a river moving in you, a joy," says the Persian mystic poet, Rumi. "When action comes from another section, the feeling disappears."

I'm with Rumi. I believe the deepest spiritual experience of music is to be found not just in listening to others make it (although there's nothing inherently wrong with that either), but in making it yourself, especially with others. And that's what we'll consider in the next chapter.

Cello

– Rigel Sauri

Musical Bench

— STEVEN. G. SMITH

Soliloquy

– Francine Gravel

3
Making Music

Half a century into this life, in the summer of my 51st year to be exact, I picked up a ukulele.

And I was born again.

Strange and wondrous as it may seem, I experienced a spiritual rebirth, new life, as I discovered the joy not just of listening to music – as I'd already been happily doing all my life – but of actually *making* it. And if I didn't make it exactly well, at least I made it with some measure of success.

More to the point, I found my greatest joy in coming together with other people to make music.

That kind of encounter hadn't originally been my goal, if only because I didn't know enough to have it as a goal. But it was my discovery, and a discovery I like to think I was led to by the Holy Spirit in the music, which American poet John Erskine calls "the only language in which you cannot say a mean or sarcastic thing."

I'm not being overly humble when I say that I have neither the natural ability nor the discipline to excel at this wonderful business of making music. There's no fear I'll ever be a virtuoso. I know this because by the time I latched on to the uke, I'd already failed at earlier attempts to play the piano, the violin, and to sing. Although I've always been a lover of music, a great listener, I'd come to accept that I would remain a lifelong non-performer.

We love music for the buried hopes, the garnered memories, the tender feelings it can summon at a touch.

– SAMUEL ROGERS

Music can be a key to unlock the safe wherein we have too often secreted our ability to be present and attentive to each eternal moment.

– John Bird

Yet some small part of me must have continued yearning to actually make music.

So the ukulele eventually caught my fancy. It's one of the easiest instruments to play. And it's relatively unobtrusive and sweet, even when flailed at (unlike either the violin or the piano). It seems to say, "Pay no attention to me; I'm just quietly strumming away in the corner. I don't need to show off or push myself into the limelight."

It started when I was 50. Midway through a family reunion in Vermont, I came back from a walk to find the gang engaged in animated conversation about a piece of music they'd just heard on the radio. "What were you listening to?" I demanded.

One of my cousins filled me in about their family trip to Hawaii the previous year. They'd taken a helicopter ride into the crater of a dormant volcano. It was absolutely beautiful, he said, but the experience was made even more marvellous by the music the pilot played for them through their headphones. It was by Hawaiian native Israel Kamakawiwo'ole.

"As we flew in over the lip of the crater," he recalled, "and the valley opened up before us, we heard this medley of *Somewhere Over the Rainbow* and *What a Wonderful World*. It was the song, he said, that I'd just missed hearing on the radio. "It was just one guy playing the ukulele and singing. We all started crying."

"All of you?" I asked.

He looked a bit sheepish. "It was beautiful," he added defensively.

Wow. My cousin is a fine fellow, but I'd never thought of him as the kind of guy who would be moved to tears over either natural or musical wonders. Besides, the uke is a bright, bouncy instrument, suited for playing happy songs, not music haunting enough to make a big, tough, exball-player like my cousin cry. I was intrigued.

With the Utmost Simplicity and Elegance

Back home at my computer, I googled Israel Kamakawiwo'ole and came up with numerous stories related to his funeral, plus reminiscences of his concerts, where it seemed people were always being reduced to tears by the beauty of his music and personality. "My knees went weak and tears started to roll down my cheeks, the aloha from this man was so powerful," wrote C. Thompson (who calls himself Brudda Bu on the Internet) about his reaction when "that giant man with his little ukulele and that golden voice, the voice of an angel," appeared on stage.

"I looked around at the audience and I discovered I wasn't alone," he added. "Everyone I saw had tears in their eyes."

Israel Kamakawiwo'ole was indeed a "giant man." His weight once reportedly reached 758 lbs (343 kg). He died in 1997, at the age of 38. But "Brudda Iz," as he is still affectionately known to many, liked to say he had a heart 10 times bigger than his body, and many apparently agreed. Ten thousand of them came to his funeral, only the third state funeral ever held in Hawaii – and the first one for a non-politician. Israel "brought a lot of attention to the ukulele, but he had a way of transcending the instrument itself," says Canadian ukulele virtuoso James Hill. And he didn't do it "in the sense of playing virtuosity or with tricks or musical back flips, but with the utmost simplicity and elegance."

Music is your own experience, your own thoughts, your wisdom. If you don't live it, it won't come out of your horn. They teach you there's a boundary line to music. But, man, there's no boundary line to art.

– Charlie Parker

A Joyful Encounter between Players

Googling Israel also brought me another surprise. I discovered a burgeoning and very supportive Internet ukulele community spread around the globe. There was a ton of help for beginners. It seems that people with knowledge and opinions on all things ukulele are quite willing to share them.

I've already mentioned how easy the ukulele is to play. For a C-major chord, for example, you just stop the first string at the third fret with any finger, then strum all four strings with the other hand.

The first time I tried that, I fell head-over-heels in love. Such a sweet and harmonious sound, light but still a full chord. Like the gui-

tar, its bigger, more difficult and more aggressive cousin, the uke is quite capable of playing harmony, rhythm, and even melody – all three at once. In the right hands, of course.

But the uke also cries out to be played *with* something – and someone – else, and it's happy to take an unassuming, backup role in any joint musical effort. It's primarily an instrument for rhythmic and harmonic accompaniment.

Soon I had joined a group of guitarists and singers, plus fiddle, clarinet, and bass, at a local café for an acoustic jam. I was surprised at how the uke's gentle sound was nearly lost amongst all the guitars, but that was actually a blessing. With my less-than-vast experience, I was missing lots of chord changes and even falling off the rhythm at times, so the less heard the better.

But none of that mattered for the time being. I was making music with other people, and even if I was the only one who could hear

Ukulele Orchestra of Great Britain

it, when I did hit the right chord at the right time, and it supported the melody line from one of the singers, or the clarinet, it felt marvellous. As harmonica player and teacher Tony Eyers asserts, "A joyful encounter between two beginning players has the same merit as a collaboration between masters. Indeed, few things match the thrill of finding your first musical soul mate." Such an experience, he adds, is "within the reach of all beginning players."

And indeed it was within my reach, as well as within the reach of my musical companions who had much more experience than me. Clearly, we all felt the same way about playing together, because nobody made a move to leave that

Music hath charms to soothe a savage breast, To soften rocks, or bend a knotted oak.

– WILLIAM CONGREVE

first evening until well after midnight. We couldn't get enough of it. After every song, we all just looked at one another and laughed out loud in wonderment at just how good this could be. It was like Canadian piano virtuoso Glenn Gould once said: "A performance is not a contest, but a love affair."

That's what this was. We weren't even performing at this stage, just jamming together. But obviously we were in love.

We were experiencing what Don Campbell talks about in *The Mozart Effect*, when he writes, "making music quickly forges strong bonds, allowing people to come together for a few precious beats of eternal time."

We continued to get together every Monday for five precious hours of jamming, which slowly evolved into rehearsals as we gradually coalesced into a real band, with arrangements and everything. I did get better, but of course I had nowhere to go but up. And I got

a louder uke. We chose a name, SwingBridge, after the bridge over the locks in Bobcaygeon, two blocks from where we first gathered, and because we liked to swing (musically, that is), and because songs have bridges, as do guitars and fiddles, and yes, ukuleles.

Simon Jeffes, British founder of the Penguin Cafe Orchestra, nailed the experience of playing with SwingBridge, for me, and I think for all of us. He said that "when someone plays an instrument you can hear their soul. Everybody gets so passionate, it's something that has to do with the relationships between us all."

I knew from that first evening of making music together with others that this was about relationships. It was about passion. And it was definitely about our souls.

"I know for me, playing music was very much a possession," explains my brother, Jeff Bird. "It was like a calling, a sense that okay, I've got to do this. There was an urgency about it."

There's music in the sighing of a reed; There's music in the gushing of a rill; There's music in all things, if men had ears: Their earth is but an echo of the spheres.

– LORD BYRON

A lifetime of making music, says Jeff, has strengthened his conviction that "our existence on earth is only a manifestation of something else much larger. I have no idea what it is exactly. Music gets your corporal existence out of the way. It distracts you. You can't think about anything else. You can't think about before and after. It's about being present in the moment. And that presence opens those doors or windows."

American writer Henry Miller once said something similar: "The moment one gives close attention to anything, even a blade of grass, it becomes a mysterious, awesome, indescribably magnificent world in itself." Presence and attention, two sides of the same coin, and music can be a key to unlock the safe wherein we have too often secreted our ability to be present and attentive to each eternal moment.

When we make music we don't do it in order to reach a certain point, such as the end of the composition. If that were the purpose of music then obviously the fastest players would be the best.

– Alan Watts

Making Music
— ELLEN DREIBELBIS

That experience of losing – and finding – oneself in the music doesn't happen often enough, admits Jeff, but over the years he's felt it more than a few times, and "once you experience it, you're hooked. It's very fleeting. There will just be moments through a night of playing when it happens. It's often when it's dangerous, when you're not sure what you're doing. It grabs you and takes you."

Toronto's Temple Sinai cantor and professional singer Gershon Silins describes those moments of spiritual connection as "very tiny." They disappear, he says, almost as soon as you notice them. But "I am successful in doing what I do," he adds, "not just if I feel spiritually connected at that moment, but if the people listening to me do."

The Secret and Spiritual Joy of Music

Veteran blues singer and guitar god B. B. King once told an interviewer how he developed his unique and powerful guitar style. He wasn't very good at playing chords, or multi-string work, he said, so he focused on single-string melody playing. Nor could he master singing and playing at the same time, so he developed a technique of singing a phrase, then echoing it, with variations, on his electric guitar (famously named Lucille). He also developed his own unique approach to playing tremolo because he had trouble mastering the slide.

So he says. I suspect, though, that B.B. King was being somewhat disingenuous in his self-assessment, since despite all these self-proclaimed handicaps, he has gone on to pioneer his own, universally admired and very much emulated, playing style. Of course, it doesn't

hurt that he has a powerful, emotive singing voice either.

But truly, B.B. King owes his success even more to the heart and soul he puts into his music making – and to the joy he clearly finds in it, and shares with his audience – than just to his musical prowess. Or, more accurately, his singing and playing owe their power not so much to his skill as to his heart and soul. This is the real secret and spiritual joy of making music.

I have seen B. B. play on two occasions and even though they were separated by about 35 years, the two shows were virtually identical in content and style. Yet there

Music is the mediator between the spiritual and the sensual life.

– Ludwig van Beethoven

Stephane Grappe

– Merryl J.

was nothing tired or forced about either performance, even though on the second occasion, age and declining health meant B. B. had to play and sing sitting down. Both times, he exuded a tremendous and heartfelt love for the music and for the people who had come to hear him.

Not surprisingly, his audience returned that love in a powerful and direct way. B. B. and his fans feed each other. It's the spiritual connection – the soul connection – that makes the music all that it is.

It's the same with Taj Mahal and with Israel Kamakawiwo'ole. And it was the same with French jazz violinist Stephane Grappelli. I have seen Grappelli perform three times, including one of his last appearances in Toronto at Massey Hall, when he was already 86 years old. At Massey Hall, a frail wisp of a man, he had to be helped out onto the stage and could only play seated. But when he put fiddle to chin and bow to strings, he seemed to become 30 again. There was a joy, a sweetness, an elegance –

and even a freshness – to his playing that has been evident from his earliest film clips and recordings, dating back to the late 1920s.

Stephane died at age 89. He kept performing, joyfully, right to the end.

Even the curmudgeonly Van Morrison (when he manages to overcome the demons that sometimes threaten to swamp him) is all about the joy and physical pleasure to be found in those old rhythm-and-blues barnburners. But then we all have our demons to deal with, don't we? Some are just more obvious than others, and in some ways I think it is music that makes all the difference in how we are able to deal with them. "I've never known a musician who regretted being one," said American composer Virgil Thomson. All the great ones exude that joy.

On the other hand, I've met countless people, mostly women it seems, who learned to play piano quite competently as children and

When I first step on the stage, it's like surfing, swimming to catch a wave. You have to work to get there, but once you do, it grabs you and you don't have to do another thing. It carries you the rest of the way. It's like riding the current in the river. There's a moment, and then, poof, I'm gone, and it's happening by itself. Some days, the current is more powerful than others; sometimes it's less powerful, and sometimes you miss the wave altogether and you have to go by remote control.

– Ann Mortifee

A bird does not sing because it has an answer. It sings because it has a song.

– CHINESE PROVERB

young teens, but who don't play anymore. Somehow, although the teaching process may have created piano *players*, it did not always encourage music *makers*. The difference between the two, according to Ward Cannel and Fred Marx in their book *How to Play the Piano Despite Years of Lessons*, is that piano players have learned how to "hit the proper note in the proper manner with the proper finger at the proper moment, properly soft or loud,"

while music makers know how to "take a tune, a melody, and turn it into a whole lot of music by knowing what [they] are doing and why [they] are doing it."

My big surprise, when I took up the ukulele at age 50, was to find that making music was not hard work, but fun. That's not what I had learned through two years of piano lessons, or 18 months of violin lessons, back in my younger days.

True, the ukulele is a more accessible instrument, but the main difference was the approach to learning. As an adult, I simply followed my nose, did my own research (made easier, admittedly by the Internet), and mostly taught myself by learning the songs I wanted to learn. I also took a few lessons from Tony Mason, SwingBridge's musical director and a knowledgeable and highly skilled guitar player who became a friend through the process of making music together. Tony figured out, along with me, how to appropriately transfer guitar

techniques to the ukulele, as the lessons became extended visits of trading licks and chords, trying different finger patterns, sharing favourite recordings and pieces of music, and figuring out how to reproduce them on the uke.

It was so much better than my piano lessons, which I recall featuring 1) music chosen by a teacher with a completely different sensibility from mine; 2) the endless repetition of scales and tuneless exercises, which I mostly neglected to actu-

ally do; 3) an automatic application of standards of "correct" technique (including rapping my knuckles with a ruler to encourage the proper finger curvature), and; 4) the occasional bout of psychological humiliation.

I'm less of a rebel than my brother, so I endured those lessons for two years. Jeff quit after one, although he now recalls it as "all those years of miserable piano lessons, of being humiliated and bored." It was a surprise to me, if not

Music is nothing else but wild sounds civilized into time and tune.

— THOMAS FULLER

to him, that he returned to music just two or three years later, with a guitar that he taught himself to play using a very similar approach I brought to the uke.

"I think it was a problem with the teaching method," he reflects now. "The whole pedagogy was about what you can't do. It was all about setting these goals. You've got Grade 2, or whatever, but you don't have Grade 3. And people would talk about it in those terms. Well, she has Grade 10 piano. There was no talk about the playing."

Even Jeff's partner, Sue Smith, a respected singer-songwriter who teaches keyboards and voice and who accompanies herself on piano – and whose musical beginnings seem almost charmed to me – was nearly driven away from the music she loved by a bad experience with

a teacher. Sue started playing piano at age three, introduced to it by her mother who loved the instrument. She began formal piano lessons at age 6, and by age 10 was also playing clarinet in her school's concert band. "I had fabulous music teachers all through school," she recalls. "I'm really lucky, and blessed that I had this great musical training. Music happens in community, and I think there is a great spiritual context to that, the connection that you share between people."

Despite this "charmed" introduction, it only took one bad experience with a piano teacher when she was in high school to set her progress with the instrument back years. She recalls that in "our first class together, he listened to me play, and he said to me: 'Have you NO technique?' I knew right then and there that piano lessons were over." It's essential, she says, to find "student-teacher relationships that work well, and that are productive."

It All Starts with a Fish

A nother musical moment, a childhood moment, came back to me recently, when I began working on this book. It was one of those formative experiences that I've been looking to rediscover or re-create all my life.

It happened one magical afternoon during my first year of school. Mrs. Felstead, my kindergarten teacher of blessed memory, told us we were "going to do rhythm band."

"What's that?" I wondered. For some reason I felt my pulse quicken.

She passed out the instruments – a metal triangle, maracas, two pieces of sanded and dark-stained dowelling she called bones, a pair of castanets, and I'm not sure what else, perhaps a tambourine. I got the dried and hollowed-out shell of a gourd with ridges cut along its belly that you scraped with the edge of a wooden ruler. It looked strangely like a fish – a name, I've since discovered, that is sometimes applied to it.

Mrs. Felstead called it a *guiro*.

She showed me how to play it. One long scraping stroke away from my body, followed by two strokes back towards me. A piece of paper came with it, with a stave and slash marks showing where and how I was to do my scraping.

I seem to recall that even at age five, and just learning the rudiments of the alphabet, I still grasped that we could convert these markings into immediate action, into music.

I was rarin' to go.

Music is by far the most wonderful method we have to remind us each day of the power of personal accomplishment.

– Chris S. Salazar

73

There followed, as I recall, what seemed to my impatient five-year-old self an interminable wait while Mrs. F worked her way slowly through the other instruments with each assigned child, explaining and demonstrating each one's part in this coming ensemble, and giving each one their corresponding musical score and instructions.

I, meanwhile, remained poised and quivering over my guiro, just waiting for the signal to let 'er rip.

Finally all was ready. Mrs. Felstead counted us in and gave the downbeat. The result was a cacophony of noise as we all raced to beat, scrape, bang, or whack our instruments, each in time to our own interpretations of the rhythm the teacher was hammering out emphatically from her desk in the middle of the classroom.

Then the magic happened. Gradually we all came into rhythm with her – and therefore with one another.

Once we had found that groove, I could have stayed with it for hours, scraping my little rhythm, and marvelling at how it blended with and complemented the other rhythms coming from my classmates, making a whole that to me was infinitely larger than the sum of its parts.

We were all grinning at one another like five-year-old fools, and groovin' to the beat – at least when we weren't focusing with furious concentration on our various instruments, trying to make sure we kept up our end of the musical bargain.

Imagine my shock and disappointment, then, when after no more than a dozen or so bars of my first taste of the magic of making music, our beloved teacher pulled the plug. I couldn't believe it. It was like being allowed a glimpse of paradise and then having it rudely snatched away.

In retrospect, I guess the school day had come to its appointed end and no doubt the teacher had other

A Very Grand Piano
– Karen Sloan

chores to do before her day was over. But at that age I was just learning about the slavery of the clock.

I now understand that what I had just experienced was an example of the wonderful Law of Entrainment first documented by Dutch scientist Christian Huygens in 1665. Huygens placed two clocks side by side and found that within a short period of time their ticking, originally slightly at odds with one another, had come together and locked up in perfect unison. Something like that had happened to me and my kindergarten colleagues in the rhythm band that wondrous afternoon.

Entraining, it seems, may be a fundamental and universal law. Two rhythms, if their sources are physically near to one another and if they are already close to one another in tempo, will invariably entrain. Who knows why? One theory says that it simply takes less energy to beat in rhythm together than it does to beat at odds.

Music produces a kind of pleasure which human nature cannot do without.

— CONFUCIUS

We begin our entraining early, in the womb in fact, as we entrain with our mothers' beating hearts. So perhaps, having begun this way, it remains our constant desire to entrain with the natural and planetary rhythms that surround us in the womb of this world – and with our sisters and brothers in whatever community we find ourselves.

Strangely, Mrs. Felstead never got out the rhythm band instruments again that year. Perhaps she found it an exhaustingly complex process trying to get a couple of dozen five-year-olds to work together. Perhaps she hadn't realized the wonderful effect that moment had on us kids. For that matter, perhaps I was the only one who found it such a magical experience.

Music as a structured
envelope of sound,
is probably the most
effective and safe
opener to the doors of
the psyche. It reaches
beyond personal
defenses to the realities
and beauties of the
person. Music gives
access to the discovery
of inner strength,
uncovers the potential
for creativity, and
manifests ways in
which life can be lived
from a center of inner
security.

— HELEN BONNY

*Concerto for a
Nightingale*
— FRANCINE GRAVEL

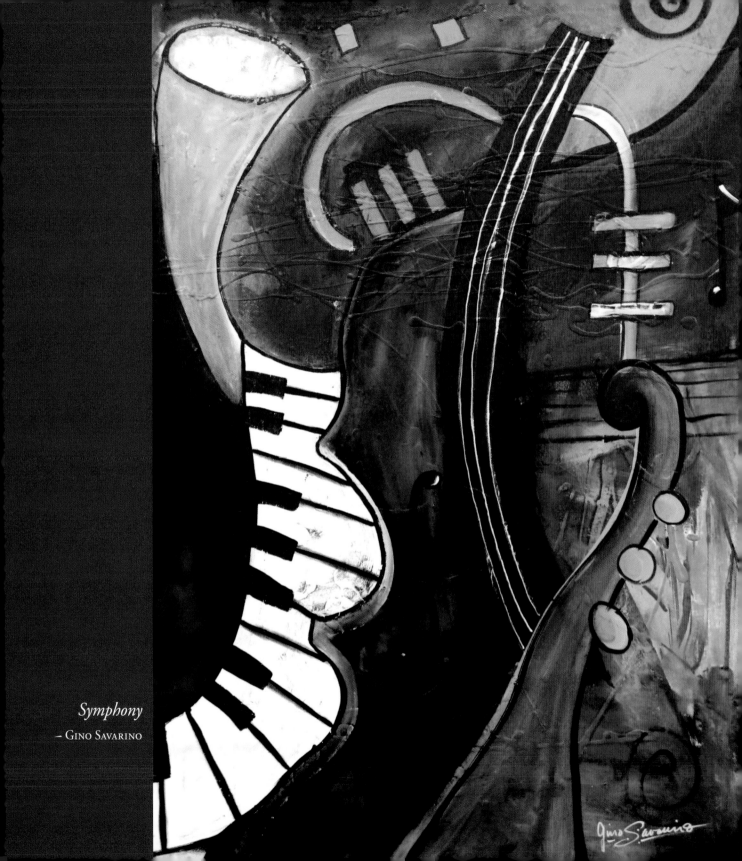

Symphony

– Gino Savarino

Integrating Mind, Body, and Spirit in a Musical Moment

Indeed, there do come moments, occasionally, when I'm playing with a band, when I will lock tightly into the rhythm and rediscover the magic of that occasion back in kindergarten. Then, for a moment, it seems I can do no wrong. Some musicians refer to it as being "in the pocket" or "in the groove." Athletes call it being "in the zone."

It can happen with any genre of music. Toronto cantor Gershon Silins describes his experience of those moments while performing his duties in his synagogue: "I can be singing and thinking about the technicalities of trying to get it right," he says, "and the immediacy of that moment becomes a spiritual thing for me. Because it works. Because I'm doing what the moment requires. Sometimes people describe that as flow, that sense of connection that's happening immediately now, where there is no past, there is no future, there is only the now."

Fledgling Inuit drum dancer Anguti Johnston told me in Iqaluit that, "when I get really into it, I don't know how to describe the feeling. It's like the music just washes over me." Perhaps it's because he is integrating mind, body, and spirit in the one musical activity. Arthur Paul Boers, a Mennonite minister and professor who wrote a book called *The Way Is Made by Walking* about his pilgrimage along Spain's *Camino de Santiago*, told Mary Hynes in a CBC *Tapestry* interview about the spiritual value of such integrated action. "We live in a culture where often a part of us is engaged, but we're not entirely engaged," he said. "We do things with our mind, or we do things with our body, or our emotions are engaged. But it doesn't often happen that everything works together

Music washes away from the soul the dust of everyday life.

– Berthold Auerbach

Celebration
– Mike Roos

at the same time." He is talking about pilgrimage, but I would say his description applies just as much, or more, to making music, when he calls it "a discipline that engages our emotions, it engages our intellect, it engages our spirit, it engages our body. And there's something very synergistic when all of that occurs together."

University of Montana philosophy professor Albert Borgmann describes music making, for those of us who love to do it, as an important "focal practice" in our lives. In an interview with David Wood in *The Christian Century* magazine, he describes a "focal thing" as anything that "has a commanding presence" in your life, "engages your body and mind, and engages you with others." And the focal practice is the actual "committed engagement with the focal thing."

Such "focal things and the kinds of engagements they foster have the power to centre your life, and to arrange all other things around this centre in an orderly way," he says, "because you know what's important and what's not." For Borgmann, the guitar is a focal thing. "It commands from me a certain kind of engagement of my body and mind. As I learn to play it (a focal practice), it engages me with the larger tradition of music and the community of musicians."

But by whatever name, that focus or centring doesn't come easily or often. Who knows what many and various factors have to be in place to conjure it? Occasionally, though, the moment will arise, the one when I will feel myself drop into the rhythmic pocket like a tumbler clicking in a lock. My chords will fall perfectly on the beat, bright and high and clean, complementing both the solid bass and drum foundation, and the leaping, swooping soloists. My volume levels will be just right. And I'll be accenting just hard enough at just the right moments, sometimes anticipating the beat, sometimes laying back.

And then sometimes, when all that comes together, Tony, our bandleader and my musical mentor, will hear it too. Amid the twanging and crashing and scraping of my fellow bandmates, he'll notice how my little contribution, unspectacular as it may be, is for that fleeting moment just right. And he'll turn and flash me a smile of absolute joy, which I, of course, will blissfully return.

It's a mutual recognition that we are, however briefly and fleetingly, communicating – with one another and with the universe – on a level that is both deeper than words and broader than the human intellect; that we are more than the sum of our parts; and that we are indeed being briefly touched by the hand of God.

My brother, Jeff, says it's about "playing with different people. You help each other. And it's usually effortless, there's no thought, or work involved in it really, with the right people."

In the end, ultimately, the music plays you, you don't play the music.

– Taj Mahal

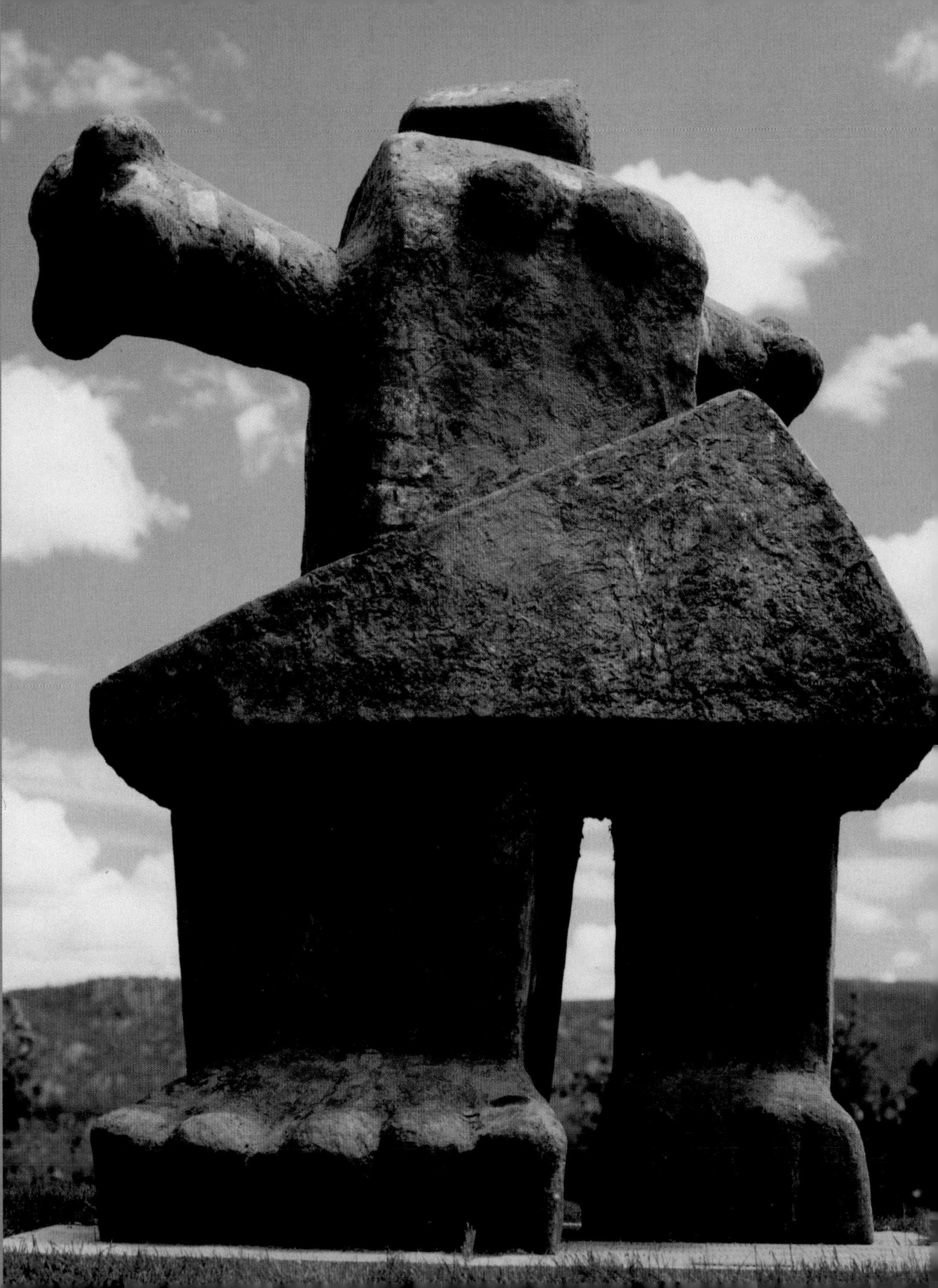

Joy

– Geert Maas

4
This Is Me

Music and Authentic Voice

In the middle of writing this book, I moved to Iqaluit, Nunavut, in the eastern Canadian Arctic, and joined the Iqaluit Community Choir.

Singing in a choir is something I'd felt a slowly growing desire to do over the last couple of decades, but the circumstances had never been quite right. Now, in this friendly and unique little city closed off from the outside world, and just entering a long, dark, Arctic winter, it seemed that perhaps the "fullness of time" had arrived.

I phoned local volunteer musical impresario Heather Daley to make inquiries. Her enthusiasm and encouragement were just what I needed. I decided to take the plunge.

Immediately, I found myself in fathoms over my head. My fellow members, and even the director, kept insisting that this choir was for anyone who wanted to sing – and indeed, there was no audition required. Instead, I was immediately signed up, given a binder full of music, and placed amongst the tenors. I soon switched to bass, closer to my limited range, but with the added danger of having fewer singers amongst whom I could hide.

I found the choral pieces these friendly people were learning terribly complex. They included *Sing a*

A song is a direct pathway into people's minds and hearts.

– Uke Jackson

New Song, by Michael Haydn (son of Franz Joseph), and a traditional and beautiful Afro-American spiritual called *Let the Heaven Light Shine on Me*, arranged by Moses Hogan.

These pieces are standard choral fare, arranged for soprano, alto, tenor, and bass. But I hadn't sung in a choir since Grade 7, four decades ago. And, at 14, I'd been more interested in teasing the girls than in singing, or God forbid, learning about singing.

I can't properly read music, to begin with. I know up from down, I understand about sharps and flats and key signatures, and I can figure out the notes, even on the bass clef, with the help of my old friends "All Cows Eat Grass," and "Good Boys Deserve Fudge Always" (although I remain embarrassingly dependent on those mnemonics). But play a low G on the piano and I'll have to warble around a moment or two before I can match it. Then, if the music directs me to jump to B flat,

I know that's an interval of a minor third, but the odds that I'll actually hit it…well, let's just say I wouldn't bet on me.

I don't do too badly if I have a strong and accurate bass singer sitting right beside me. After years of singing in church, I've learned to follow someone else reasonably well. But if he sings a wrong note, I'm likely to follow him right down that garden path, and if the other basses happen to be away that evening, it's pretty well guaranteed I'll end the song singing along with the tenors, even if I started out on the bass part.

I hadn't been singing with the choir long before I started to have dreams – or more accurately, nightmares – about singing. I dreamed one of my best friends, who'd played in a rock band as a teenager, tricked me into coming to the front of the "class" at a singing workshop. There, in front of everyone, he insisted I demonstrate a particularly complicated tune by singing

The mind and the voice by themselves are not sufficient.
– MAHALIA JACKSON

my bass part, knowing full well I couldn't do it. I woke up in a sweat, my heart pounding.

This nightmare nearly came to life one evening at choir practice when no other basses showed up and we were learning a new song – Oscar Peterson's *Hymn to Freedom*. I hunkered down into my shirt collar like a frightened turtle, while director Peter Workman took first the sopranos, then the altos, and finally the tenors, through their various parts. There was only one part left, the bass – me. Peter turned to me and said, "I won't make you go through this all by yourself in front of everyone. Get Lorraine (my wife, the accompanist for the choir) to help you with it during the week." Phew. I'd already come to appreciate Peter's direction, but with that one statement he earned my love and loyalty to the grave.

The fish in the water is silent, the animals on the earth are noisy, the bird in the air is singing. But [people have in them] the silence of the sea, the noise of the earth and the music of the air.

– RABINDRANATH TAGORE

The total person sings, not just the vocal chords.
— ESTHER BRONER

Peter calls choral singing a trust relationship. "I've always found trust to be important," he says. "You have to trust what the director tells you. If you do what the director says, it's going to work. It's going to sound great, and you're going to be so pleased, which is good for you."

Of course, the director has to prove him or herself worthy of that trust.

Conducting choirs is "a blood-pressure-lowering, health-altering experience," continues Peter. "It's a complete release for me." If the choir does "a really good job, I'll start to cry. I'll end up with tears streaming down my face. It's not sadness. It's a joy, or a connection. Everything lines up. The harmonics and the overtones are there. And choral music has the power of the connection of multiple people. It's a case of 'where two or three are gathered...' and 'the whole is greater than the sum of the parts.'"

So why do we sing? Well, as the black southern gospel quartet, the Harmonizing Four, vocalize on an old record in my collection, "I sing because I'm happy, I sing because I'm free." Sue Smith, a singer-songwriter and music teacher based in Guelph, Ontario, offers a variation to that. "I sing because it makes me happy," she says.

Blues singer B. B. King says that, "singing about your sadness unburdens your soul." Peter Workman says singing connects him with "a larger whole," both the wider world of humanity and a spiritual world

beyond. "I would say that it puts a truer self together. You can't be false in music. You can't fake it."

All of these are deeply spiritual responses.

As compared with playing an instrument, says Sue, singing is "immediate, and present and authentic. It's coming from deep inside your body. You are the instrument; you are in the driver's seat. It's such a joy to be inside a song that you really love and that has a beautiful melody, and important, meaningful words. To be inside of that, phrasing it and responding musically to what's going on in the moment… it's a great joy."

Sue Smith also teaches singing, which she considers "a very spiritual practice. You have to be guided by the best intentions, and you have to allow the best intentions to move through you, to help this person come authentically to their voice."

When she teaches, she says, she may make suggestions and offer metaphors for what the voice

should be doing, "but if I actually sing with the person, the learning is usually immediate. There's this immediate resonance between singing voices. It's fascinating. That's a deep, intimate communication."

I sing like I feel.
— ELLA FITZGERALD

> *It is the nature of babies to be in bliss.*
>
> — Deepak Chopra

As research for her Ph.D. thesis at York University, Victoria Moon Joyce, a singer and writer from Toronto, asked a wide variety of people why they sang. The responses, later published in *Bodies That Sing: The Formation of Singing Subjects*, often reveal, she says, "the deeply symbolic meaning that singing represents":

to feel a sense of freedom… to fly… to abandon myself… to connect with the stars… to reach out to others… to give myself… to feel better… to create beauty… to give praise… to express myself in ways that words cannot… to be truly seen and heard… to connect with my children… to comfort… to touch the divine.

Of course, there were also other, more self-serving responses: "to score chicks… to stand out from the crowd… to be rich and fa-mous." Yet even those responses are in some way about meaning and identity and self-affirmation, albeit at the expense of others, which is clearly a suspect motivation from a spiritual point of view.

Our voices are such an intimate mirror of who we are, body and soul. "From its first coos and moans, the baby expresses its being and consciousness through its voice," says Don Campbell in *The Mozart Effect*.

A baby can bawl and whine for hours, and its cries convey the incredible power that it knows to be its self. Utterance then becomes the pathway to self-knowledge, self-naming, and self-respect – as well as self-hatred. The voice, in many ways, is the most exposed "organ" of the body.

As with the voice, so, doubly, with singing, which is clearly our most intimate form of music making. It is the most mysterious, the most powerful, and the most personal. When we sing, our whole body resonates with our voice, in a tone and a timbre that is unique to each of us, and unique to each moment in time. We may tighten up and block the resonance to degrees, out of fear, embarrassment, or shame that we aren't good enough or can't sing – as so many of us have been told at some time in our lives. But even the nature of that shutting down will be unique to each of us and to each occasion.

We delight in the beauty of the butterfly, but rarely admit the changes it has gone through to achieve that beauty.

– Maya Angelou

Alas for those that never sing, But die with all their music in them!
– OLIVER WENDELL HOLMES

Talk about mystery. To start with the most basic question, just how do we manage to make our voice hit a particular pitch? With the piano, it's simple. If you want the G above middle C, you just have to know which key will give you that note. Even with the violin, I know – more or less – where my finger should go on the D string to give me that G. Even if I rarely get it just right, at least I know there's a specific spot on the fingerboard that will give me the G I'm looking for.

But with the voice, it's all about vocal chords deep inside the throat, and the echo chamber that surrounds them. Tightening the vocal chords just the right amount, and changing the shape of the chamber as needed, is totally a matter of feel – and no vision. Mysterious…

and as intimate as you can get.

There's no escaping the voice as an expression of the self. Whatever we're feeling about ourselves, good or bad, the voice will reveal it to those who are paying attention. As Jessye Norman, the powerful African-American opera diva, puts it, "Singing is, for me, a spiritual, emotional, physical and intellectual expression of my breath." That's what singing is for all of us, really. And that's why most of us limit our singing to moments when we're sure we're alone, perhaps in the shower or in the car. Unlike Jessye Norman, we're not *divas* – a word, incidentally, with the same root as *divine*.

In 1985, my father and I took a canoe trip together east of Peterborough, Ontario. We spent a couple of days in the sunshine on a small, gentle river. I'm so glad we did it, because he died suddenly and unexpectedly a year later.

But I hope my dad was glad, too, because I remember I spent the whole two days singing two or three songs from Bruce Springsteen's *Born in the USA* album, over and over. Why? Well, mainly because in one of the songs, which were mostly about lost love, Bruce sings about being *"laid off at the lumber yard."* One silly little line. But my father had owned a small lumber yard when I was growing up. I had worked there as a teen, every Saturday and in the summer. I'd even gone on to work in other lumber yards and in construction.

I *identified*, in other words. I felt Bruce was singing about my own working-class youth, even though, with my dad as the boss, I happily missed the experience of being laid off. (This speaks volumes – or sings volumes – about how powerful an experience it is to find your own reality reflected in the words and emotions expressed in a song – even when it's just one little phrase.)

I wanted to sing these songs, perhaps because it seemed a way to tell my father that working in the lumber yard had been important to me, that I valued it and valued him. So sing I did, at length and at volume. (Canoeing down a river in the woods is good for that.) My poor, long-suffering father, true to his lovely personality, never breathed a word of complaint. I hope he got the message, somehow, that this was a homage to him, however clumsy and even subconscious my presentation.

I always wanted my music to influence the life you were living emotionally - with your family, your lover, your wife, and, at a certain point, with your children.

– Bruce Springsteen

Muddy
Smile
– Reesa Dawn
Jacobs

COMING FOR TO CARRY ME HOME

I t's the singers we remember, of course, and the singers we seek out to meet so many of our musical needs. An instrumental dance number can be wonderful, powerful fun, and a symphonic passage deeply moving, but add the human voice singing human poetry and the music becomes that much more memorable and accessible. You heighten the experience tremendously.

Some of the most powerful, beautiful and moving examples that North America has produced of the human voice singing human poetry come to us from this continent's most oppressed people. It is a simple but deep music, born of pain and suffering, and it is music to stir and strengthen the weariest soul.

In 1619, the first boatload of 22 Africans, captured into slavery from various countries and tribes in their homeland, were sold in Jamestown, Virginia, to white colonists. Thus

One good thing about music, when it hits you, you feel no pain.

— BOB MARLEY

Bob Marley

— TRAVIS CELLAN

The history of a people is found in its songs
— George Jellinek

began almost two-and-a-half centuries of slavery for African-Americans in these British colonies and in the new nation of America. Forbidden to make or own musical instruments while in bondage, the people turned to their own, intimate, powerful voices to "express their pain, anger, grief, faith, and joy," says an essay on <u>africanamericanspirituals. com.</u> "Just as Africans communicated among themselves using drum language in their own countries and tribes, so did the enslaved Africans continue to do in America by using 'cries,' 'hollers,' 'calls,' 'shouts,' which eventually evolved into spirituals and work songs."

When those slaves encountered the gospel story, mainly through the work of Baptist and Methodist evangelists, they responded from the heart to its message of liberation, and to the hymns of composers like Isaac Watts. They applied their own African musical traditions to those European hymns and turned them into something new and even more powerful. Spirituals like *Wade in the Water, Nobody Knows the Trou-* "still cause people today to examine themselves, tap their toes, clap their hands, shed tears, laugh, dance and shout," says the African-American spirituals website. "In its original form the spiritual was free in form, rhythm, text, and performance styles and allowed for much variation from singer to singer as it was passed on orally. Such characteristic features are typical and unique to the Negro [*sic*] Spirituals."

The memory of things gone is important to a jazz musician. Things like old folks singing in the moonlight in the back yard on a hot night or something said long ago.

— LOUIS ARMSTRONG

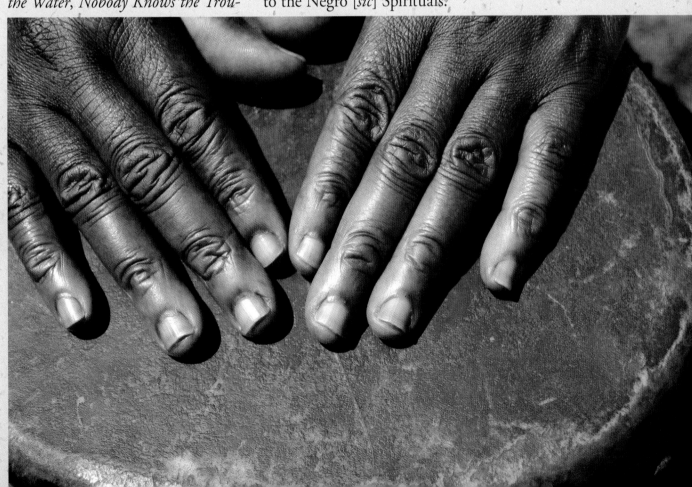

Bruce Cook, in his book *Listen to the Blues*, says the spirituals were already well-known before the Civil War, and "since the ministry to the slaves did not really get under way until fairly late in the eighteenth century, it seems to have taken the blacks no more than about 50 years to master the style of the white man's hymns, alter it, and develop a whole body of their own sacred music."

I recall a period when some intellectuals tended to dismiss spirituals for reflecting a colonialist, pie-in-the-sky, theological fatalism, the effect of which, they claimed, was to maintain slavery's status quo. It seems clear now, however, that there was much more to these beautiful songs. They were songs of faith and resistance. "The basic idea of the spirituals," says James H. Cone in his book, *The Spirituals and the Blues*, is that slavery contradicts God; it is a denial of his will. To be enslaved is to be declared nobody, and that form of existence contradicts God's creation of people to be his children. Because black people believed that they were God's children, they affirmed their somebodiness, refusing to reconcile their servitude with divine revelation.

Despite barriers to communication between slave communities, purposefully maintained by the slavers to increase the slaves' powerlessness, the spirituals spread quickly by sung word of mouth throughout the entire African-American slave population, perhaps, writes Cook, because of "the 'secret' message of protest they contained. For it has come to be rather generally recognized that when the slaves sang, 'Let my people go,' they were thinking less of the Israelites in captivity in Egypt than of themselves in captivity in America."

Another fascinating aspect of these beautiful, sacred songs is that many of them also carried coded messages to help slaves escape their captors and make their way north to the Free states and Canada. The spiritual *Follow the Drinking Gourd*, for example, encourages escapees to head north by following the North Star as indicated by the Big Dipper constellation – the drinking gourd.

Wade in the Water instructs escapees to walk through creeks and rivers to throw the bloodhounds off their scent, because "God's gonna trouble the water."

"Sweet Canaan, the promised land," refers to the land across the "Jordan River," which for those African-American slaves meant the Ohio River, a northern boundary line for the slave-holding states. The chariot in *Swing Low, Sweet Chariot* was a metaphorical reference to the Underground Railroad, "coming for to carry me home" to the freedom land across the Jordan/ Ohio River. Fleeing slaves would be carried there by the volunteers of the Underground Railroad – "a band of angels, coming after me, coming for to carry me home."

The sweet sound of those marvellous spirituals, born of an authentic encounter between people suffering some of the most heinous oppression imaginable, and their living God, has permeated Western society – a marvellous, free-will gift from the authentic voice of African-Americans to the whole world. The effects of this music continue to be felt, directly or indirectly, by us all.

You can cage the singer but not the song.

– Harry Belafonte

I've said that playing the blues is like having to be black twice. Stevie Ray Vaughan missed on both counts, but I never noticed.

– B. B. KING

There is nothing more glorious than a powerful singer in full-throated flight, hitting the high notes and letting the crescendos ring out in all their emotive wonder – especially when the words and the music make a profound and intimate match. When words, music, voice, and person combine well, they can create an experience that is, as Peter Workman notes, much greater than the sum of its parts.

"The way we read words on the page is related to how we speak," says Sue Smith. "When we sing, we

extend all of our vowel sounds, so the sound of the word is changed. It's extended through time, and the experience of reacting to it is a different experience. You have more time in the word. So the comprehension of the word changes."

Sometimes the words may be extended so much that they are no longer identifiable as words. Listen to Van Morrison's live version of *Listen to the Lion*, for example, from his double concert album of 1974, *It's Too Late to Stop Now*. Van's lyrics, at first presented in a fairly clear, straightforward manner, gradually evolve into growls and barks and extensions of word fragments. But the effect that Sue describes remains the same, only exaggerated. We spend even longer "in the word," or in the sounds, which are still the echoes of earlier enunciated words. When it's carried off well, as in Van's song, the effect can be mesmerizing. Many blues and gospel singers do the same, as do operatic singers, for that matter.

Blues-rocker Janis Joplin provides another prime example, although both Van's and Janis's vocal extensions can be traced back to the original African influence carried forward in America through spirituals, blues, and gospel music.

Whenever I hear a recording of Janis singing something like *Ball and Chain*, or *Summertime*, I get a lump in my throat and my eyes start to leak. Even as a naive teen, I knew there was something about her that was special. But Janis's tragic death by heroin overdose on October 4, 1970, at age 27, threw everything she had done into a new light. And with the limited understanding that comes with age and experience – and with the possibilities that audio and visual recordings allow for review, reflection, and reconsideration – the real tragedy of her life becomes even more apparent (I would even say transparent) in her singing.

I saw Janis perform once, in Toronto just months before she died,

Audiences like their blues singers to be miserable.

– Janis Joplin

during a cross-Canada train tour of pop/rock heavy hitters, known as the Festival Express. In 2003, a documentary film of the concert series was finally released on DVD, with excellent footage of Janis performing both *Cry Baby* and *Tell Mama*. Janis's performance of *Tell Mama* is nothing short of heartbreaking for its power and raw emotion. One reviewer described her as "light and energy and joy itself in nearly every frame" of the film, but I don't see that at all. I hear a powerful cry from the depths of a soul that, with the clarity of hindsight, I now believe was desperate to the point of self-sabotage for human connection. I see a lost young woman presenting with disarming honesty – as a gift – her deep, deep need for love. It's a moving and frightening performance because we all will recognize and appreciate, if we're honest and in touch with our own depths, the common humanity in her cry. We all share it, to some degree.

My mother is Welsh. She grew up in Cwmafan, a small mining village in the South Wales coal valleys, near the various hometowns of poet Dylan Thomas, actor Richard Burton, and singer Tom Jones. The Welsh take great pride in their oratorical and singing abilities (and oratory itself can almost be considered a form of singing, existing as it does at the edge where the spoken and the chanted word meet). Welsh male-voice choirs from those mining valleys have travelled the world.

Yet my mom is convinced that she cannot sing, that somehow she missed the Welsh gene. I'm not sure where she got that idea – because to me she has a lovely voice – but school, church, and/or family would be the likely culprits. It's such an oft-repeated story.

In Western society, writes Victoria Moon Joyce in *Bodies That Sing*, singing is about expressing the self in its most heroic aspect, the solo voice being unique and analogous to the rugged individual, the suffering soul, the prophetic lone voice crying from the wilderness (of savagery), the star (in the darkness). Perhaps one of the reasons why so many adults feel they cannot sing is because they measure themselves in individualistic terms in a cultural climate where singing is…about individualized talent, giftedness and performance. Afraid to appear inadequate, incompetent, uncultured, unhip, or otherwise inappropriate and not good enough, they decline and withdraw.

If you can walk you can dance. If you can talk you can sing.

– Zimbabwe Proverb

Many adults, she suggests, can't "think of singing as an activity that they can just play with and enjoy socially without the anxiety of being judged." So it may be with my mom, perhaps – and with many people. I know that's generally the way of it with me.

For me, it may have started in Grade 3. Our teacher, whom I adored, had taken great pains to mould us into a class choir, eventually to compete in the local choral-music competition sponsored by

the Kiwanis Club. At that point, as now, I loved singing in the choir. It was the connection thing that Peter Workman speaks of, and the experience of the whole being greater than the sum of the parts, my thin voice contributing to a great, roaring whole, powerful and complex, and with overtones and harmonics to make it come alive. And, if truth be told, I loved singing for my teacher, strove to please her by belting out the words with great gusto. I was looking forward to the choral competition.

Then, when the great day came, in the middle of a last classroom warm-up just before we were to march down the hall to the auditorium and mount the stage to give our performance, my beloved teacher singled out three or four of us and suggested that we not sing with our classmates today. Instead, she told us, "Just move your lips and mouth the words."

I didn't blame her for that – she was my teacher after all – and I was still at an age to believe she knew everything. I just concluded that I must not be a very good singer.

I don't blame her now either, although I probably could have become at least a competent singer if she had given me a little more encouragement, instead of worrying about how her class was going to fare in a small-town competition. But she was only human after all.

With many things, but perhaps especially with something as intimate, soulful and creative as singing, our self-esteem balances on a knife edge, ever ready to be tipped over into the abyss of "I-can't-do-it land." The tragedy is that so often the negative message can come in a casual aside, spoken, or even just intimated, without any thought or realization of its possible consequences.

I rarely sang again – and never solo – in a public or performance setting after that experience in Grade 3. I still sang when I was alone in the woods or in the car. And I joined my voice with oth-ers while hidden deep within the congregation at church, though for a long time I did little more than move my lips, for fear of aggravating the minister, or worse, the choir director.

But gradually, over the years, I have increased in volume, determined (at least when I'm confident I know the tune) to reclaim my voice and my right to exercise it in song. Now, on a good day, and with a good tune, I fairly belt out those hymns.

Because the good news is that it's never too late, as long as we can draw breath, to let our soul express itself in song.

Tibetan Singing Bowl

"I have songs in my head from so many languages and people. I know my sound is in the middle of this whole."

— Taj Mahal

When I was growing up, though, I thought that whole thing about the Welsh and singing was just a myth. Then I took a trip to Wales, to visit my "Welsh rellies," as my brother and I like to call them. I've got half a village of them in Cwmafan, it seems. One night, about two dozen of us, all related, gathered at the home of one of my cousins for a visit. Beer all around, chat about old times, and stories for me about when my mom was a young girl growing up there. Then someone suggested a song and the evening took off.

Nearly everybody sang, unashamedly and unselfconsciously. They sang with clear, strong, open voices; and they sang in key. They sang solos and they sang together. They sang in unison and they sang in harmony. They knew so many songs by heart: light opera, especially Gilbert and Sullivan; hymns; pop tunes; folk songs;

classical lieder. I was stunned. They weren't all great singers, but they were all competent, pleasant, and expressive singers. They knew how to sing, and they weren't shy about doing it.

They weren't in Jessye Norman's league, of course. How many of us are? But when I think of that evening, I recall a comment she made: "My voice is a very good friend to me. We've become very close over the years, and now when I ask my voice to do something for me, it does it."

That's how it felt for me listening to my Welsh cousins. That's how, belatedly, I would like it to be for me. I would like my voice to be a very good friend.

My uncle Stan was there that evening, too. He was a short, powerful boulder of a man who had spent his working life down in the coal mines. I remember being quite frightened as a young child, when I met him just come home from the mine. He was dressed in trousers and a sleeveless undershirt, originally white, but now streaked, like his face and arms, with coal dust and sweat, and he greeted me with a fierce scowl.

I watched him during this night of song, sitting quietly in the corner, the patriarch of the gathering. He won't sing, I thought to myself. Not this gruff, gravel-voiced rock of a man who was still a little intimidating to me, even though his personality had sweetened considerably once he no longer had to make those daily trips to the coal face in the bowels of the earth.

But after a while, someone said, "Give us a song, Stan," and while he raised his hand in protest at first, others soon took up the cry until, with a small smile of recognition, he acquiesced, perhaps partly in honour of the guests from Canada. The room grew quiet as he took a few deep breaths, straightened his spine, closed his eyes and began to sing *Song of Songs*, in a pure, powerful baritone voice. I didn't know the song, but it was beautiful and his singing of it was a revelation to me of a completely new aspect of the man. I think that's what he wanted to show us.

Robert Plant

– KAREN YEE

OUR HOME AND NATIVE LAND

It was another year, another Mariposa Folk Festival on the Toronto Islands. It had been a beautiful, hot, sunny summer day, with just enough breeze blowing off Lake Ontario to keep the day from becoming too sweltering, especially if you could find a spot on the grass in the shade of one of the big willow trees.

In the gathering dusk, I joined the long lineup of festival goers to catch the last ferry boat back to the mainland. Once on board, I headed up to the open top deck, where I discovered two young men, armed with guitar and mandolin, leading the rest of the passengers in a sing-along. They were in the middle of Bob Dylan's *Blowing in the Wind*, and I happily joined in (but quietly, in the background, of course). We went on to Steve Goodman's *City of New Orleans*, then the campfire favourite, *Kumbaya*. By then someone must have been feeling the need for some Canadian content, because they launched into Ian and Sylvia Tyson's *Four Strong Winds*.

We sang sweetly and softly, as I recall, with the city lights of the downtown office district beckoning us across the water, and the buildings themselves silhouetted against the deep, deep blue of the late evening sky. It felt right, somehow, to be singing of heading out to Alberta. We were Canadians after all, most of us anyways, and we were glad to remind ourselves that we had our own songs.

As *Four Strong Winds* ended, we all fell into a quiet reverie, pondering

A song will outlive all sermons in the memory.

– HENRY GILES

what to sing next. Something else Canadian seemed in order. So much of the day had been devoted to Americana roots music, which was wonderful, but not our own. Then, some long-haired, sandalled genius quietly started up a tune all the Canadians on the boat knew well:

"Oh Ca-na-da, our home and native land…"

There was a collective, not-quite-silent gasp. The national anthem? This was the early '70s. We were folkies! We weren't going to sing some jingoistic, patriotic song we'd had to stand for and groan along with every morning of our school-going lives.

Somehow, though, it seemed right. By the third line, we were singing along: "With glowing hearts, we see thee rise, the true north strong and free…." There were no swelling trumpets, of course, no snare drums rat-a-tat-tatting out a marching rhythm. This was no militaristic reading of this normally pomp-

and-circumstance-laden national anthem. Instead, we sang it quietly, gently, as befit a ferry ride in the gloaming and in the sweet evening air at the end of a fine day of acoustic traditional music from backwoods hollows and lonesome hillsides.

In that moment, it became a new song, a reflective song of thanksgiving for the gift of this beautiful country and its many riches, which we shared: its freedom and tolerance, the beautiful of its varied natural landscapes, its cultural variety. And we sang our song of thankfulness for all the music we had heard that day, and for all the music we could find around this beautiful country – and beyond – or could even make ourselves, together.

That moment encapsulates, for me, the spiritual aspect of singing:

thanksgiving, celebration, intimate self-expression, togetherness, connection...

As Thomas Dorsey, the father of African-American gospel music, once famously put it, "Say Amen, somebody."

Money doesn't make the man. Some people have money, and some people are rich.

– Thomas A. Dorsey

5

Do You Wanna Dance?

It's a frosty January evening in Peterborough, Ontario – a Saturday night – and the parish hall of St. John's Anglican Church is about ready to explode with a surfeit of noise, heat, and movement. Music and the sound of laughing voices and stomping feet pours out of the open side door like a cloud of steam into the frigid night air. The 100-plus-year-old building and its mother church sit on a downtown hilltop, overlooking the Quaker Oats plant and the Otonabee River. Behind the church and hall sits the old courthouse and jail, once nicknamed Johnson's Hotel in song by local musical wags, after the magistrate who regularly assigned them rooms there.

Tonight, dance callers Myra Hirschberg and Tom Calwell are holding one of their regular "contra dances" in the parish hall. A hundred or so red-faced, sweating, giggling souls are hopping up and down, and swinging their partners hither and yon as a fiddle-and-banjo string band in the corner hammers away at the classic *St. Anne's Reel*. To the casual observer, it looks and sounds like chaos, and despite the best efforts of Myra and Tom, it often is.

Contra dancing is a bit like the square dancing you might have tried at some point in primary or secondary school. It's done "in sets of couples, to jigs and reels or

The moment in between what you once were, and who you are now becoming, is where the dance of life really takes place.

— Barbara de Angelis

113

southern old-time tunes," explains Tom. But you change partners with each repetition of the 32-bar tune, until you've danced with all the other dancers in your set and have returned to your original partner. The caller teaches the sequence of moves for each dance before the music starts, and then calls those steps out for the dancers as the music plays, "to keep everyone moving and dancing together."

With the string band keeping a simple, steady beat throughout each dance, which can last as long as 15 minutes or more, Tom or Myra call out a series of instructions, like "ladies chain, allemande left, swing your partner, circle right" (not necessarily in that order, mind you).

That's the theory. In practice, the instructions come awfully thick and fast. And since modern contra dances make a point of encouraging people of all ages and all levels of experience (including none) to participate, it's not uncommon to have confused dancers grabbing you by

Nobody cares if you can't dance well. Just get up and dance.
– Dave Barry

the arm when you least expect it and attempting to swing you where you don't want to be swung. That's a good time to keep your sense of adventure, and to recall the words of famed choreographer Agnes de Mille: "The moment one knows how, one begins to die a little. Living is a form of not being sure, of not knowing what next or how. One leaps in the dark."

Perhaps that's why the most confused dancers are often the ones having the most fun. At least they'll be the ones giggling the most.

To really understand contra dancing, you have to try it, says Myra. "It's where you'll find people having the time of their lives, and where you'll quickly realize that if you can walk, you can dance. You get to smile, hold hands, swing, and share a good experience with someone who may have been a stranger, but has now become a friend." By the end of the evening, you'll likely have danced with everyone in the room. And perhaps you'll have helped embody the words of Irish poet William Butler Yeats in *The Fiddler of Dooney*:

> For the good are
> always the
> merry
> Save by an evil chance
> And the merry love the
> fiddle
> And the merry love to
> dance.

About 17,000 years ago, on the limestone wall of a cave in southwestern France, someone painted the image of a dancing figure dressed in the skin of an animal and playing an early form of stick percussion. Popularly known as *The Dancing Sorcerer,* the pictograph is one of our earliest records of the human commitment to music and dance. Dance has been with us a long, long time.

Once we learned how to "manipulate noise rhythmically," Grateful Dead percussionist Mickey Hart explains in the book *Drumming at the Edge of Magic,* one of the first things we did was to "use it in our sacred dance." We made "sacred noise, rhythms created from the sounds found in the materials we had at hand – wood, bone, stone, animal skin, assorted gourds and pods, plus the human body itself, which scholars like [James] Blades and [Curt] Sachs generally assumed was one of the very first instruments."

As Hart also pointed out to the U.S. Senate hearings on the elderly, "our bodies are multidimensional rhythm machines with everything pulsing in synchrony, from the digesting activity of our intestines to the firing of neurons in the brain."

No wonder we have to dance; it's in our very guts – and in our spirits. It's sacred.

So dance we do. Every culture, every race, every age has danced… and does dance…and will dance.

When I was in my early 20s, there was a flurry of multicultural activity in the cities of Ontario. A number of cities started springtime festivals to celebrate the many peoples who had come to Canada from around the world to build new lives in the postwar immigration boom. As the multicultural festivals were meant to showcase, these immigrants greatly enriched life in Canada.

Churches and cultural societies from many of these ethnic groups organized "pavilions" for the festivals, where they featured the history, food, crafts, and music of their own particular countries of origin. In Toronto, the event was called Caravan, and in Oshawa it was called Jubilee. I also joined in the jollity at festivals in Kingston and Guelph.

The food and the drink were great, of course, but by far the best fun was to be found in the music – and especially the dance. What a gift, to be able to watch and even participate in so many different styles of dance during an evening of pavilion crawling, from church hall to school gymnasium to a big tent in the park. In the course of those festival evenings, I danced to the intoxicating rhythms of Trinidadian steel drums, Ukrainian accordions, Irish and Quebecois fiddles, Scottish bagpipes; Greek bouzoukis (long-necked, stringed instruments similar to a lute or mandolin), Peruvian charangos and Brazilian cavaquinhos (sisters to the ukulele), West African djembes and Cuban conga drums.

The music that speaks most directly to my own particular soul, it seems, is almost always about the dance, because my soul is seated firmly in my body – at least for the duration of this earthly existence – and my body, being a body, wants to move in conscious, rhythmic celebration.

The one thing that can solve most of our problems is dancing.

— JAMES BROWN

Try this the next time you're out for a walk. Put a little dance in your step. It doesn't have to be grand or elaborate. Just think of a rhythm or, even better, a tune that more or less matches the speed of your walk. Then add a little swing to your stride to suit the music. Or as Taj Mahal might say it, "Put a little shake in your shaker, a little quake in your quaker, a little romp in your stomp." Swing your hips from side to side. Add a little up-and-down motion – a hop – to your step. Pump your arms. Bob your head. You might find that it helps to hum, whistle, or even sing the tune under your breath, depending on circumstances. I know that, for me, this exercise raises my energy level, lifts my spirits, makes the world seem a little less forbidding. It's also good

for my body; it gets me breathing a little harder and my heart pumping a little faster; it increases my metabolism and my circulation. And it works every time.

While you're at it, you might want to breathe a little prayer of thanksgiving for the gift of your body (whatever its shape), for the simple gift of embodiment, and for the possibility of dance, however active or physically limited you may be. Even a barely perceptible head bob or an eyelash flutter can qualify as a form of dance.

One of my all-time favourite fictional heroes is Alexis Zorba, or Zorba the Greek, for whom music and dance is a vital part of being alive. I love the scene at the end of the movie, when, with their grand get-rich/local-economic-development mining scheme in shambles around them, Basil (played by Anthony Hopkins) turns to Zorba (played by Anthony Quinn) and

says simply, "Zorba, teach me to dance."

Zorba's eyes flash with excitement, as if saying, "Finally!" Then he kicks off his shoes and there, on the empty sand beach, they dance out the joy and tragedy of life.

We've been on a long journey with these two by now, and we recognize with a start that this is the best possible reaction to the chaos and loss they've been through. It's one of the most spiritual dance moments I know.

Joy

– Geert Maas

119

Of course, the dance isn't just in our genes; it's also in our jeans, since we all know that much of dancing is about sexual energy and courtship. As the witty and acerbic Anglo-Irish playwright George Bernard Shaw liked to say, "Dancing is a perpendicular expression of a horizontal desire." The corollary to that is the folk saying by our old friend anonymous: "Dancing is the most fun you can have with your clothes on."

With all that physical – and sexual – energy flashing around in dance, I supposed it isn't surprising tha t some of the more sexually repressed among us have at times considered dance evil. Take the Puritans, for instance. In 1632, William Prynne pronounced this judgment on the delightful activity:

Dancing, is, for the most part, attended with many amorous smiles, wanton compliments, unchaste kisses, scurrilous songs and sonnets, effeminate music, lust provoking attire, ridiculous love pranks, all which savour only of sensuality, of raging fleshly lusts. Therefore, it is wholly to be abandoned of all good Christians.

And I can't resist including this little piece of purple prose, from an 1892 publication written by T. A. Faulkner and entitled *From the Ballroom to Hell*.

But, let us turn our attention again to the dancers, at two o-clock the next morning. This is the favorite waltz, and the last and most furious of the night, as well as the most disgusting. Let us notice as an example, our fair friend once more.

She is now in the vile embrace of the Apollo of the evening. Her head rests upon his shoulder, her face is upturned to his, her bare arm is almost around his neck, her partly nude swelling breast heaves tumultuously against his, face to face they whirl on, his limbs interwoven with hers, his strong right arm around her yielding form, he presses her to him until every curve in the contour of her body thrills with the amorous contact. Her eyes look into his, but she sees nothing; the soft music fills the room, but she hears it not; he bends her body to and fro, but she knows it not; his hot breath, tainted with strong drink, is on her hair and cheek, his lips almost fierce, intolerable lust, gloat over her, yet she does not quail. She is filled with the rapture of sin in its intensity; her spirit is inflamed with passion and lust is gratified in thought.

With the last low wail the music ceases, and the dance for the night is ended, but not the evil work of the night.

*Life is like Tango...
sad, sensual, sexy,
violent and quiet.*

– Anonymous

The Dancers

– Jean-Baptiste Carpeaux

Now I know that people bent on manipulating and taking advantage of others – or those bent on being taken advantage of – can certainly use music and dance as tools for their own nefarious ends (to take a leaf from the writing style of Mr. Faulkner). But let's not put the blame on dance itself, which I and many others would argue is one of God's wondrous gifts to us.

Sue Smith, is, as I've already mentioned, a fine singer-songwriter and piano player who also teaches music. For Sue, it was dancing that ended a painful, decade-long musical dry period, and that helped her start playing and singing again.

"I started studying dance," she says. "I took classes. I had to learn to be in my body in an authentic way and dance was the way for me to do it. In retrospect, I was coming to understand my body, how I exist in a physical presence, how my soul exists in my body. I was training myself through dance to be present in music.

"I spent many years studying all kinds of dance: Martha Graham modern technique, Argentine tango, salsa, contact dance… and through that I got to know myself in a new way. I was becoming healthier and happier, knowing that it was safe to be here in this body, and to be involved in this musical activity, to let music move me through dance."

Argentine tango remains one of her favourites. "It's all about really intense communication between two people," she explains. "It's improvised, you know. And it's through the body. There's no talking. You don't talk, you just feel it. It's profound."

Lucille Krasne, who founded a weekly tango club that meets in the summer in New York's Central Park by the statue of Shakespeare, would

I do not know what the spirit of a philosopher could more wish to be than a good dancer. For the dance is his ideal, also his fine art, finally also the only kind of piety he knows, his "divine service."

– Friedrich Nietzsche

Dance is the hidden language of the soul of the body.

— MARTHA GRAHAM

evidently agree. "I don't know if tango breaks or heals hearts," she says. "But it is about making a connection."

British writer and psychologist Havelock Ellis held that "dancing is the loftiest, the most moving, the most beautiful of the arts, because it is no mere translation or abstraction from life; it is life itself."

Dance "is as close to God as you

are going to get without words," says Judith Jamison, artistic director of the Alvin Ailey American Dance Theater.

I would argue that dancing can take you even *closer* to God than words can do. I'm a writer, so I love words. I have great respect for their power to move the mind and touch the soul. But dance… dance engages the mind, the soul, *and* the body. It's more holistic; it goes deeper than words, right to our very guts and bones, to those places where the rhythms originate – where life originates. I have no doubt that when we dance, God smiles. Or, as the title of a documentary film by Les Blank of a 1960s "love-in" suggests, *God Respects Us When We Work, but He Loves Us When We Dance.*

Blank has made many other excellent documentaries about older dance traditions, including *J'ai Eté au Bal/I Went to the Dance,* about the Cajun dance music of Louisiana; *I'll Sprout Wings and Fly,* about Appalachian fiddle-based dance music; and *Always for Pleasure*, about the tradition of New Orleans street parades, which are basically mobile outdoor dances. The titles themselves make it clear how Blank feels about his subjects, but here is his further description of the New Orleans parades.

The presence of a band in the street in New Orleans is an open invitation to all to join in and dance along, no matter how rich or poor, or what color the skin. The people dancing along with the band are called the "second line" (the first line being the band itself), and they come from their houses or bars or places of work when they hear the music coming.

Like a sudden, cooling rain shower when it is insufferably hot and humid, the unexpected second-line parade affords a welcome opportunity to take off that coat and tie, or leave an ailing, nagging wife or unpayable rent notice or whatever else is holding a person down, and to get out in the street and dance it all out. I also liked that many of these spontaneous non-funeral parades had no destination and no apparent purpose except immediate pleasure.

At the other end of the continent, in the eastern Canadian high Arctic, we find Anguti Johnston, a young Inuit man who is part of the revival of his people's tradition of drum dancing. Often, the drum dancer will perform solo, but sometimes several will perform together. In these performances, the drum dancer sings and dances at the same time, accompanying himself or herself by beating on a large frame drum. In this way, the drumming itself is an integral part of the dance. The drumming *is* the dance.

To watch us dance is to hear our hearts speak.

— Indian Proverb

And we should consider every day lost on which we have not danced at least once. And we should call every truth false which was not accompanied by at least one laugh.

— Friedrich Nietzsche

It's fascinating to see how the process of recovering this dance tradition has also helped many Inuit people rediscover pride in their culture and identity. The dance is a powerful, healthy, and growing alternative to the temptations of substance abuse for young Inuit men and women.

"There were times when I didn't want to put down my drum," says Anguti. "I just wanted to dance all night. Sometimes we did drum dance for very long periods – six or seven hours in a night. I'm really, really happy after. I think maybe it's the reconnection to my ancestors."

It's What They've Come For

From my position on the stage in the back row of our band SwingBridge, I watch as Tony bobs his head, eyes half closed, mentally counting the beat through a couple of bars to make sure he's got the tempo just right. Then, in his down-home southern drawl, he announces the song for the audience: "Here's a little thing called Route 66, and it goes a lot like this." He launches into his patented, wind-up guitar lick, and we all jump in on the downbeat. The song goes roaring off at breakneck pace.

Route 66 is always one of our last songs of the evening when we're playing a dance, often the very last one before the encore we hope we'll get called back for, when we'll bring it down sweet and soft with that old Tin Pan Alley classic, *I'll See You in My Dreams.*

Tonight it's a wedding, and the revellers have been up and boogying with enthusiasm all evening.

They're hot and sweaty, but still eager for more, still beaming with anticipation. As soon as we kick in behind Tony's intro, they're off and stomping. They can't help it – and they don't want to help it. This is what they've come for.

The great thing about it is that these dancers are all ages, from barely past the toddler stage to grandparents on the verge of re-entering the toddler stage. There are aunts and uncles and cousins by the dozens, plus many long-time family friends. They're dancing together in celebration and as part of this public ceremony of joining and commitment between a man and a woman, whom they care for deeply.

As always, seeing – and feeling – people respond so physically to the band, puts an extra snap in our playing. With each verse, we seem to be winding up just a bit more, both the band and the dancers as we feed off each other. We're not

There is nothing in the world so much like prayer as music is.

– William P. Merrill

playing faster, they're not dancing faster. We're just playing (or dancing) *harder*. It's difficult to describe, but it's about intensity and accent. We're anticipating the first beat of each measure just a little, creating a syncopation that gives the music a little more rhythmic drive.

We're not backing away from the offbeats, but we're hammering harder on the downbeats to emphasize the difference between the two. It's a wonder strings haven't begun to snap and fly by now. And to be honest, we've turned up the volume – although that's not always a good thing, and we've been known to go too far down that questionable road and end up in the swamp.

Not tonight though. This is one of those rare, wonderful nights when everything seems to be working. The dancers are matching us in intensity, too, stomping their feet harder, raising their knees higher, leaving the ground just a little bit further behind with each hop. I know we can't keep this up for long, neither dancers nor players.

Then Tony kicks into his guitar solo. He starts low and simple with a repeated series of triplets on the low E-string, then gradually winds it up with a progression of ascending runs that climb higher and higher up the fretboard, each run more extended and rapid-fire than the previous one, like a range of mountain peaks where each peak surpasses the last.

The whole thing reminds me of those hand-cranked sirens that start with a low hum and grow louder and higher as you turn the handle faster and faster.

I glance to my left. Bruce's fingers and thumb pick are flying as he rolls out a repeating rhythmic riff at the bottom end of his guitar. Al's wrists are a snapping blur as he raps out the rhythm on the snare drum with his brushes. They both catch my eye at the same time and flash smiles of delight. Al's excitement and joy is threatening to overwhelm him – it's funny to think that he's a United Church minister. Bruce, as befits his personality, is a bit more restrained, but I can tell he's in heaven despite himself. Ted, his thinning hair drawn back in a ponytail, has his eyes closed as he throws in those delightful bluesy guitar fills at the end of each four-bar line.

Over to my right, Rob is hunched over his bass like a heron, his index and middle fingers rumbling on the thick strings. He looks dangerous but happy; this is as close to rock and roll as we get. Eileen, who gets a break from singing on this song, is flashing her tambourine and dancing right out on the front edge of the stage. And George

When we are dancing we are not aiming to arrive at a particular place on the floor as in a journey. When we dance, the journey itself is the point, as when we play music the playing itself is the point.

– ALAN WATTS

is poised with fiddle under chin, bow raised, his left hand dancing in anticipation on the fingerboard. He's waiting for the chord changes to come round to the beginning again, when it will be his turn to let fly with a screeching, soaring solo of his own.

As Mark Twain once remarked, "We consider that any man who can fiddle all through one of those Virginia Reels without losing his grip, may be depended upon in any kind of musical emergency."

Out on the dance floor, which is simply a patch of grass under a canvas roof set up by the side of a lovely lake, the dancers are a confused melee of waving arms, pumping legs, fly-ing hair, and shaking hips. I see a five-year-old girl hanging on to her grandpa's hands for dear life while he dances her around the room on the toes of his once-polished shoes.

And everywhere smiles. We're all in this together, making big communal music. The dance is the music and the music is the dance. We're experiencing the kind of communion and oneness in this wedding dance that is all the bet-ter for being such an occasional and special event.

And as a member of the wed-ding band, I get to contribute to someone else's celebration; to be integral to it, in fact. It's a won-derful privilege, and I consider it a sacred trust.

"Dance," said Edward Demby, "is a little insanity that does us all a lot of good."

When words leave off,
music begins.
– HEINRICH HEINE

Bluescape

– Rigel Sauri

Flautists

— Geert Maas

6

A Joyful Noise

THE MUSIC OF SPIRITUALITY

It was a song that triggered the major spiritual rebirth in my life, a rebirth that brought me reluctantly, and even now at times still waveringly, back to the Anglican Church I grew up in. That rebirth has coloured my career choices and my writing, and indeed all aspects of my life, for three decades now.

It wasn't even a complete song that triggered the sea change. It was just two short lines from a reggae tune called, appropriately, *Spiritual Revolution*, by the Jamaican band Third World. The lines were these:

Every man has a conscience,
   every man's got a soul
Worth much more than silver,
   worth much more than gold.

Third World was the scheduled opening act for a Toots and the Maytals concert I attended at Toronto's Massey Hall in 1981. But Toots was held up at the border for some reason, and Third World, a band I was totally unfamiliar with at the time, became the evening's only act.

They blew me away that night. Even today, when I think back on

The only proof you need that there is a God is music.

– KURT VONNEGUT

a lifetime of concert going, that experience stands out as one of the best. Third World had a sound that was tight and professional, and that mixed roots reggae with a smooth, almost Motown groove. The band combined great harmonies, lots of dynamic range and tight rhythmic ornamentation, with a theatrical and at times gymnastic presentation. Their songs were soulful and, at the same time, sensual, joyful, sometimes political, and even cerebral. For me it was a winning combination.

I went out immediately the next day and bought one of their albums, *Journey to Addis*, which didn't disappoint me at all. Six months later I bought their newest release, *Rock the World*, which has a "north" side that sounded more like American soul music, and a "south" side that was basic dub and reggae.

I liked it all from the get-go, but I loved the reggae side, which was very funky, even though the overt spirituality challenged me.

For some reason, those two lines kept rattling round and round in my head, working their way down deeper.

I'd had a pretty "churchy" upbringing, in a small, working-class, low-Anglican community, and overall it had been a warm, supportive experience. I'd also been working for a Catholic publication for a couple of years, which had allowed me to meet and interview some wonderfully spiritual people whose own faith had helped them stand up for justice in long, exhausting, and sometimes pretty dangerous struggles. People like Cesar Chavez, founder of the United Farm Workers in California. Or like a young, indigenous Filipino man who was organizing his isolated and oppressed fellow tribespeople in his homeland. Or like the mothers (and wives) of the disappeared in Guatemala and El Salvador, some of whom had fled their countries after repeated threats and even attempts on their own lives.

Yet despite all that, I had convinced myself that I was an atheist. I wasn't anti-religion. I just figured spiritual belief was for those who lacked the intellectual courage to face a world without the crutch of some kind of God (oh, the arrogance of youth).

But these Rasta musicians in Third World didn't seem weak to me. Nor did Cesar Chavez, or the mothers of the disappeared. Nor, for that matter, when I got around to thinking about it, did my own mother and father, who were also people of deep faith.

I'd also just finished reading Tolstoy's novel *Resurrection*, and was in the midst of devouring his collection of essays The Kingdom of *God Is within You*. Looking back on it, I was pretty clearly in full-blown seeker mode.

It all came to a head on the Labour Day long weekend, on a bus ride from Toronto to Haliburton (where I had lived the first year of my life). A rainstorm had just swept through, and, as the bus turned

north from the Lake Ontario plain and began climbing the hills of the Oak Ridges moraine, a blustery wind was keeping everything stirred up. The lowering evening sun lit the thrashing grass and curling leaves from beneath, and all of creation seemed to shine "like shook foil," as English Jesuit poet Gerard Manley Hopkins once phrased it.

I think music in itself is healing. It's an explosive expression of humanity. It's something we are all touched by. No matter what culture we're from, everyone loves music.

— BILLY JOËL

137

I'm a country boy at heart, and I'd been too long stuck among asphalt and high-rise buildings. So I was in ecstasy as I watched the scene unroll outside the bus window and as I contemplated the weekend ahead in the Haliburton bush. And I still had those two lines from the Third World song rolling around my head: "Every man has a conscience, every man's got a soul, worth much more than silver, worth much more than gold."

I know I have a conscience, I thought. It plagues me constantly. But do I have a soul? Or is that just my fearful self wishing it were so?

Then, as I gazed out the window at the beautiful rolling hills shining before me, and as Third World's music echoed in my inner ear, it became suddenly and completely clear to me. Of course I have a soul! Every man, every woman, every child, and indeed every living thing has a soul. Perhaps even the very stones have souls.

My fearful self, I realized, had not been wishing it were so, but rather, had been wishing it were not so, hanging on to the idea that we have no souls. That part of me wanted to go on living a comfortable, middle-class life, with all its material compensations and distractions. It wanted not to have to think about eternity and morality, about my relationship with and responsibilities toward the rest of the world around me, my connection with an overarching spiritual power, a prime mover, God.

Immediately and strangely, as this understanding dawned, I felt a powerful presence descend upon me – upon the very soul whose existence I had been doubting just moments before. This "presence" seemed to envelope my soul, my essence, in a warm, velvety and comforting darkness that, surprisingly, made me think of the wings of a giant bat (surprising because a bat would never before have been a comforting image to me).

It wasn't an entirely comfortable feeling then either. My first reaction was, Oh no. I don't want this. I don't want to be "born again" and have to go out and thump a Bible and preach to people on street corners.

And immediately I felt, with a deep pang of regret and loss, the withdrawal of that presence. I knew at once that I had been offered an immeasurably valuable gift – and that I had rejected it.

But with that withdrawal there also came a message of forgiveness and patience to assuage the pain, and I heard/sensed a message something along the lines of this: "My dear child. I love you. You know I would never force on you anything you don't want. Just know that I am with you always, and I will love you always, without condition."

It was a beautiful experience and a wonderful message. It changed everything for me, from that day to this. And music played a key role – music with a spiritual basis, music created and performed with a clear spiritual intention.

Country music is three chords and the truth.

– Harlan Howard

139

We All Drink the Same Water

Who could retain a grievance against the man with whom he had joined in singing before God?

– St. Ambrose

As I hope I've made clear throughout this book, I love all kinds of music. I love a good love song, whether it's about the pleasures of love, or about its sorrows. I love a good dance tune, whether it be an old-time reel on the fiddle, an accordion-driven Cajun two-step, a klezmer freylekhs, a South African township jive, or a rockabilly boogie. I love a crashing allegro movement from a symphony, and a heartbreaking operatic aria. And I love an upbeat call to social change, like Jimmy Cliff's *Meeting in Africa*.

To me, they're all spiritual, because they're all about life – the joys and sorrows of life, the rhythms of life moving in body, mind, and soul.

Yet so often, the most moving music, the music that can fill my heart full to overflowing – with joy, with passion, or with yearning for the promised commonwealth of God – is music that is overtly and unabashedly spiritual in its basis and intention. I'm talking about songs of praise to God, hymns to creation, and songs of thanksgiving for all God's gifts to us; songs calling for God's justice to come and overturn this sorrowful world of human-made injustice, as well as songs crying out to God for clarity and closeness amidst confusion and despair.

When I use the word God, here, I do so as a kind of a shorthand for the eternal, the spiritual, the divine essence, the creative force – which we can approach through art and metaphor (including and perhaps most sublimely, through music) – but whose true nature remains

ultimately beyond our imperfect comprehension. The word God, itself, is a metaphor.

I once heard a traditional Plains Cree elder explain that we all drink the same water, from the same spiritual aquifer. We just use different cups, different cultural containers, to access that water. That, for me, describes the way it is with spiritual music.

I may respond just as strongly to Mahalia Jackson singing an African-American spiritual like *Steal Away,* as I do to four young Siksika (Blackfoot) men pounding out a powerful rhythm on the big drum and singing an honour song in tightly pitched falsetto voices. Or maybe it will be the close harmonies of a bluegrass-tinged southern gospel piece like *I'll Fly Away* that will move me, or sitar virtuoso Ravi Shankar's meditative interpretation of a sacred raga from the Hindu tradition. It could also be a Wesleyan Methodist hymn sung in a slow, keening wail by an elderly Ojibway congregation accompanied by an ancient, wheezing pump organ; or a group of Rastafarian Nyabinghi drummers singing a chant in praise of Jah. It might even be the

Rattle. Ca. 1880. Wood, string, H. 29.2 cm (11-1/2 in.); Diam. 15.2 cm (6 in.). The Crosby Brown Collection of Musical Instruments, 1889. (89.4.1963). Haida, British Columbia, Canada. The Metropolitan Museum of Art, New York, NY, U.S.A. Photo Credit: Image copyright © The Metropolitan Museum of Art / Art Resource, NY

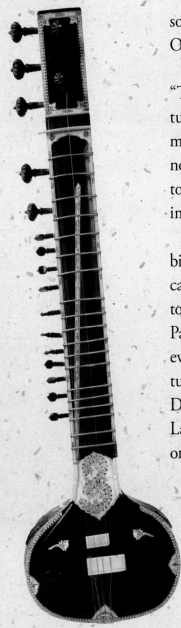

sonorous harmonies of a Russian Orthodox choir.

As Shankar himself has said, "The highest form in music is spirituality." Opera singer Jessye Norman is convinced that singing does not only happen on earth. "It has to happen in heaven. I can't imagine heaven without singing."

"Down in New York we have a big Russian Cathedral," the American mythologist Joseph Campbell told a gathering at San Francisco's Palace of Fine Arts, during a 1986 event called "From Ritual to Rapture, From Dionysus to the Grateful Dead." Here's a further excerpt from Lawrence Gerald's transcript, posted on his website at www.sirbacon.org.

You go there on Russian Easter at midnight and you hear "Kristos Anesti!" Christ is risen! Christ is risen! It's almost as good as a rock concert. It has the same kind of life feel. When I was in Mexico City at the Cathedral of the Virgin of Guadeloupe, there

it was again. In India, in Puri, at the temple of the Jagannath – that means the lord of the moving world – the same damn thing again. It doesn't matter what the name of the God is, or whether it's a rock group or a clergy. It's somehow hitting that chord of realization of the unity of God in you all. That's a terrific thing and it just blows the rest away.

Hindu musician and spiritual leader Sri Chinmoy said that when "musicians play soulful music" and "singers sing soulfully," they will be bound to awaken the consciousness of the audience. After all, each individual who comes to listen to songs or to hear music comes to get something abiding – the lasting joy that inspires them to see and feel something in themselves that is absolutely new and unprecedented – unprecedented joy, unprecedented love.

Music Will Bridge Any Gap

Virtually all religious traditions – except perhaps a few isolated sects whose exception proves the rule – value and make use of music in their spiritual practices. Music and music-making are crucial to the maintenance of distinctive belief systems, say authors Philip V. Bohlman, Edith Blumhofer, and Maria Chow in their book *Music in American Religious Experience*. Vanderbilt University professor Gregory Barz describes "a vibrant sacred soundscape" that "exists in America's churches and synagogues, often in our own backyard."

I do not see any reason why the devil should have all the good tunes.

— Rowland Hill,

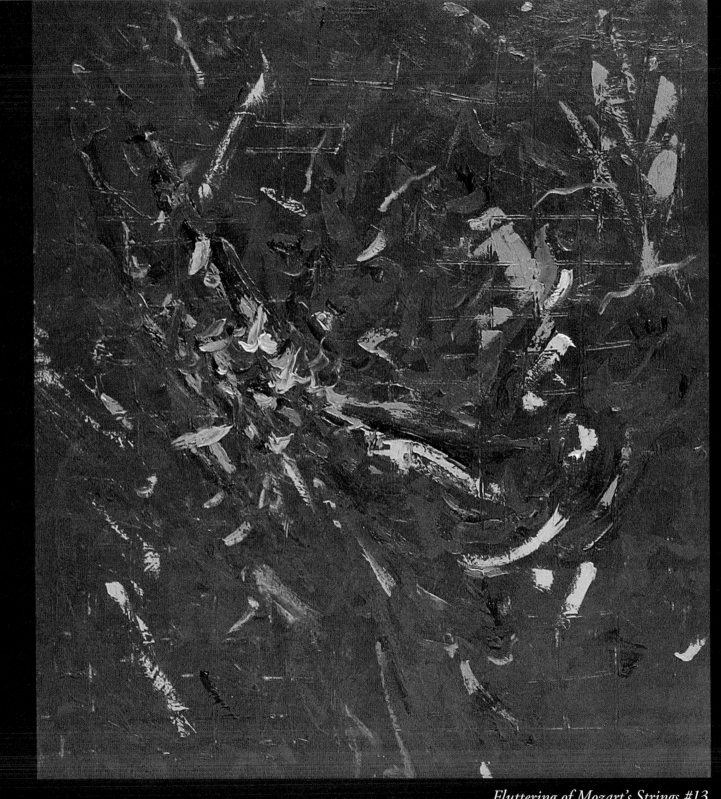

Fluttering of Mozart's Strings #13
— JULIA TROPS (PRIVATE COLLECTION)

"I don't see religion surviving without having music in it," says Iqaluit choral director Peter Workman. "Music connects at a different place in your brain. It'll bridge any gap." Workman sometimes finds himself disagreeing seriously with the theology of one preacher or another. "But I can accept that we're all different. I can accept it because of the music," which undergirds and informs everything that happens in the church.

It can be a heady and stimulating experience to discover moving spiritual music from a tradition that is brand new to you. I think of the music of Yukon Dene singer/songwriter Jerry Alfred, and of the ethereal Qawwali singing of the Sufi master Nusrat Fateh Ali Khan. But it's often the familiar music rooted in childhood that stays with you through a lifetime and that offers the deepest, ongoing spiritual resonance.

As I said at the beginning of the chapter, I was raised in a small, humble and nurturing low-Anglican congregation in southern Ontario. My first musical memories from that church are of singing children's hymns with three dozen other freshly scrubbed and combed boys and girls in the basement Sunday school, at St. John's Church, Port Whitby.

Lines like "Jesus loves me, this I know, for the Bible tells me so," wedded to simple tunes we could all sing together, had a mysterious power to move my heart. Even now, five decades later, they continue to move me and to call up memories of polished wood, stained glass, a piping organ, and, thankfully, a community of caring people.

I believed those songs then, and I believe them now.

Of course, I like to think my spiritual life has grown a little more sophisticated, a little broader in its embrace, but the basic foundation was laid there and then, in those songs.

You need music. I don't know why. It's probably one of those Joe Campbell questions, why we need ritual. We need magic, and bliss, and power, myth, and celebration and religion in our lives, and music is a good way to encapsulate a lot of it.

— Jerry Garcia

But who can fathom which hymns, particularly, will stir the individual soul, and why. *This Is My Father's World* has long been a favourite of mine, and continues so, even though I no longer understand God to be in any way limited to, or best imaged by, the male gender. To me, it seems that this hymn weds an uplifting, traditional English melody to poetry (by American Presbyterian minister Maltbie Babcock) that does a lovely job of celebrating the beauty of creation. And the United Church of Canada, in its hymnal *Voices United* has dealt with the gender issue by changing "my Father's world" to "God's wondrous world." This change meets a theological need, which is important, but the hymn also loses a little of its sentimental, emotional power for me, which comes with singing familiar words that remind me I am a beloved child of God:

This is God's wondrous world,
And to my listening ears
All nature sings and round me
   rings
The music of the spheres.

This is God's wondrous world,
I rest me in the thought
Of rocks and trees, of skies and
   seas,
God's hand the wonders
   wrought.

This is God's wondrous world
The birds their carols raise.
The morning light, the lily
   white,
Declare their Maker's praise.

Similarly, in the Anglican liturgy as practised in our little church, there was one canticle we used only rarely, but which seemed to speak to me beyond all others. It was called *Benedicte, Omnia Opera* or *The Song of the Three Children*, and

146

I can remember my excitement on those rare Sundays when we'd actually get to sing it during the service. Again, it was the creation aspect I responded to and, I think, the idea of so many different parts of the natural world all joining together to praise their Creator. Let me share a few lines as we sang them:

O ye Sun and Moon, bless ye
the Lord.
O ye Stars of Heaven, bless ye
the Lord.
O ye Showers and Dew, bless
ye the Lord.
Praise him, and magnify him
forever.

And a little later,

O ye Wells, bless ye the Lord.
O ye Seas and Floods, bless ye
the Lord.
O ye Whales, and all that
move in the Waters, bless ye
the Lord.
Praise him, and magnify
him forever.

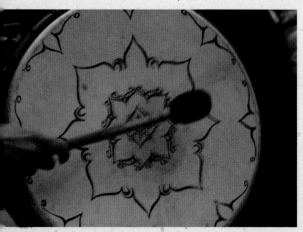

Similarly from his own childhood, Laverne Jacobs, an Anglican priest, church organist, and member of the Bkejwanong First Nation (Walpole Island), recalls with great affection the "revival meetings" that used to take place in his and other Aboriginal communities. "We sang some of the old Methodist hymnody, but in the Ojibway language," he explains. "They also have their own rhythm. If you've got a classically trained organist or pianist, they would have difficulty following that rhythm. There's something innate, which is Aboriginal. The rhythm is of the people."

If you've been fortunate enough to hear Aboriginal communities sing these hymns yourself, in their own language, you know that there is truly something else going on besides a good old Methodist hymn sing.

"There would be a regular circuit," says Jacobs. The gatherings would be held at "Walpole, Sarnia, Moraviantown, Kettle Point, Mount Pleasant (Michigan), and all the way up through the Michigan peninsula. People would go from one camp meeting to another."

The meetings were almost always "held in the bush. The people would erect a tent or some kind of arbour, and it would be very evangelical. But what stuck out was the singing in Ojibway. It would go on all night. You could hear the singing throughout the whole community. There's something about those songs, those Ojibway songs, that really touched people."

The Ojibway language has declined significantly in recent years in Bkejwanong, says Jacobs, although a movement to revive it

All deep things are song. It seems somehow the very central essence of us, song; as if all the rest were but wrappages and hulls!

– THOMAS CARLYLE

is now gathering strength. Unfortunately, the tradition of Ojibway hymn singing has faded even more. "Most of the people who knew the old songs are gone. We have one woman now who carries the memory and who knows all the hymns. She'll sing, and I'll try to play it by ear, and we do it until I get it right."

Laverne Jacob's brother, Allen, is part of a trio of men who are committed to saving the Ojibway hymns. The Back Settlement Band has already put out one CD of recovered songs in the Ojibway language, performed in a limpid, reflective style, sparely accompanied by guitar, mandolin, and dobro, almost like the sound of water droplets dripping one by one from an overhanging tree branch into a springtime forest pool. These are the soulful hymns that the men remember their parents singing at home, at church services, and in the camp meetings. A second CD was nearly ready to be released at the time of this writing.

Jacobs is clear. The music and the singing of those camp meetings engendered some of the most powerful experiences and memories in his early spiritual life.

The most evocative part my own early faith life was the traditional "Festival of Lessons and Carols" we always celebrated at St. John's, on the last Sunday of Advent before Christmas.

The tiny church was packed as we sat waiting excitedly in our pews (I speak for myself as a young boy). The ushers made their way up and down the aisles, lighting candles set atop head-high, alternating red and green poles that had been erected at the end of the pew rows for the occasion. When all the candles were ablaze, the church's regular lighting was switched off, bathing us all in the magical glow of candlelight.

Music is either sacred or secular. The sacred agrees with its dignity, and here has its greatest effect on life, an effect that remains the same through all ages and epochs. Secular music should be cheerful throughout.

— JOHANN WOLFGANG VON GOETHE

The organist introduced a series of minor chords, and we lifted our voices together in the mournfully expectant phrases of "O Come, O Come Emmanuel...and ransom captive Israel, that mourns in lowly exile here, until the son of God appear..."

The choir processed up the aisle, their voices strong behind us at first, then sweeping ahead and bouncing off the front wall of the sanctuary as they passed us, faces and white robes glowing in the candlelight like so many angels. The thundering sound of the organ and a church full of swelling voices seemed almost to shake the old stone church on the chorus.

"*Rejoice! Rejoice! Emmanuel, shall come to thee, O Israel.*"

As a child, I knew how music could bring the walls of Jericho tumbling down.

We settled into our seats, then, for the first reading of the Christmas story from the gospels, rising after each reading for another carol: *O Little Town of Bethlehem, Away in a Manger, Hark the Herald Angels Sing, Good Christian Men Rejoice, While Shepherds Watched Their Flocks by Night.* And ending, of course, with *Silent Night.*

You can always argue with the theology behind those old-fashioned carols – and I may well find myself agreeing with your arguments. But for me those musical Christmas services were more primary than theology. Through communal singing, they brought metaphors and stories to life, and gave me a deep, direct, and emotional experience of my Creator. They enriched my spiritual life immeasurably.

The Music Calls Us Home

It was the last night of a week-long healing gathering for Aboriginal people dealing with a vast array of community and personal pain and dysfunction, the legacy of a still-unfinished colonial process. All week long, about 100 of us had gathered in a Métis conference centre on the southwest shore of Lake Winnipeg, to share stories and drumming, to laugh and cry together, to move a little further along the healing path, and to build relationships across language, cultural, religious and even racial barriers. As a representative of the Anglican Church's healing project on residential schools, I was very privileged to be the only non-Aboriginal person there. I had discovered that I, too, had a lot of healing to do, and I had taken steps along that road along with everyone else at the gathering. It had been a profound and moving week.

But now the official program had come to an end. Tomorrow we

would all leave this place and one another, as we went off to various home communities, mostly across the province of Manitoba. And so we had gathered one last time in the warm, early summer darkness outside the conference centre, where elders had been tending a sacred fire for us throughout the week.

There was some joking and kibitzing, but mostly reflective silence, as we sat around the fire gazing into the flames. Then, quietly at first,

People who have problems today, they will listen to this music. And this music will come and will stop their heart, and will help them to go through the problems they are facing.

— Njacko Backo

one voice on the other side of the circle started up the hymn *One Day at a Time, Sweet Jesus* – a favourite among Christians in groups like Alcoholics Anonymous and other addiction treatment programs.

I was surprised to discover that nearly everyone joined in and knew the words not only to that song, but to several similar hymns that followed. I knew full well, after a week with these people, how many had wrestled – and were still wrestling – with addictions, the origin of which often lay in residential schools traumas. I was mostly surprised at their sense of connection to these Christian songs, given the church's negative role in causing these traumas, and given the strong emphasis during the week on the recovery of traditional Ojibway, Cree, Saulteaux, and Dene cultural and spiritual traditions – an emphasis we had all mutually and enthusiastically embraced.

I was moved, too, to see these people apparently reconciling within

themselves two traditions that have so often historically been antagonistic towards each another. Certainly, I knew many instances when the churches had been antagonistic – and oppressive – towards traditional Aboriginal practices and beliefs. As a result, those recovering their traditions often now harboured justifiable feelings of anger and resentment against the church.

But here, once again, music was playing an important role in the reconciliation, cutting to the heart of the matter and helping wounded hearts to open.

A few hours later, my roommates and I were awakened in our beds, in the first grey light of a beginning dawn, to the sound of drumming and chanting coming in through the open window. We hastily pulled on shirt and jeans and stumbled barefoot outside and down towards the lakeshore, from where the sounds were coming.

From the edge of the 10-foot bluff along the shore, I could see

I have my own particular sorrows, loves, delights; and you have yours. But sorrow, gladness, yearning, hope, love, belong to all of us, in all times and in all places. Music is the only means whereby we feel these emotions in their universality.

– H. A. OVERSTREET

*Music was my refuge.
I could crawl into
the space between the
notes and curl my back
to loneliness.*

— Maya Angelou

the four young Dene men who had been sent down by their community at Manitoba's northern edge to participate in the healing gathering. They were standing waist-deep in the silver-grey waters of Lake Winnipeg, facing the east-

ern horizon, where a fiery red line marked the spot where the sun was just about to appear. Each held a hand drum, caribou skin stretched across a willow hoop frame, with a twist of dried sinew strung loosely against the inside of the drum so it would rattle when the skin was struck. All four were beating in time, in a rapid and simple, syncopated sequence, as they chanted in urgent, high-pitched voices, calling out a descending series of tones they repeated over and over.

Around the drummers, spread out at a little distance, were other Cree, Ojibway, and Saulteaux participants in the healing gathering, also standing hip-deep in the lake and chanting towards the horizon with outstretched arms, greeting the rising sun with thanksgiving and celebration for the gifts of creation and life, and for the possibility of healing.

I watched in awe and in tears as the sun gradually crested the horizon, and the light of the world broke over

the day. And I was reminded of an Ojibway woman in Sioux Lookout, Ontario, who had been raised in a residential school, cut off from the traditional big drum of her people. When she finally heard it, she said, "It felt like going home."

There was something in the sound of the drum that called her – called her home. And so it was with me that morning – as so often. The music calls us home, to the beating heart of love.

He who sings scares away his woes.

– Cervantes

Arpeggio

– ALEX FONG

Conclusion

And so we end where we began – with the recognition that music accompanies us on our entire journey through this life. It provides the rhythmic underpinning to which we can dance or trudge (as circumstances may seem to require) along our daily journey. Personally, I recommend dancing whenever possible – even when it may seem near impossible. Remember Zorba.

Listening to music, whether alone or communally, can enhance our periods of prayer and meditation on the deep, unknowable mysteries of life, God, and spirit.

Making music can take us out of our worries about past, present, and future, and help us stay right here in the rhythmic pulse and eternal wonder of the cosmic moment. Making music with other people can connect us with those others at a level of intimacy that goes far beyond what words can express.

Singing can be our most intimate and personal form of musical expression, as we generate sound from deep within our bodies, and inhabit words and poetry in ways that enhance meaning and integrate both body and mind.

Dancing to music (even if it's only chair dancing) helps us connect with our bodies, and through our bodies with the earth, the natural world, and all things physical (all things bright and beautiful).

Ritual songs of praise or thanksgiving to our creator can focus our worship and deepen our faith lives almost more than any other spiritual practice.

It comes down to Mickey Hart's assertion that music and rhythm are in our bones and our genetic makeup. Not just in the air we breathe, but even in the rhythmic way we breathe it. As Alexander Smith says, it is in our very natures to "blossom into song, as it is a tree's to leaf itself in April."

As musicians/healers, it is our destiny to conduct an inward search, and to document it with our music so that others may benefit. As they listen to the music coming through us, they too are inspired to look within. Light is being transmitted and received from soul to soul.

– KENNY WERNER

THESE ARE A FEW OF MY FAVOURITE THINGS:
RECOMMENDED LISTENING, VIEWING, AND READING

There are so very many more I would like to include, and the list keeps changing, but here are some recordings, films and books that have stuck with me over time; all available as downloadable singles on I-Tunes.

RECORDED MUSIC

Anders Osborne – *Stuck on My Baby*

Baka Beyond – *Eeya Be (Elephant Song)*

Bob Stewart – *Fishin' Blues* (Featuring Taj Mahal)

Bruce Cockburn – *Wondering Where the Lions Are*

Buena Vista Social Club – *Chan Chan*

Choir of Westminster Abbey, Ely Cathedral & Gerald Gifford – *Brother James' Air*

Czerwinec, Grabowiecki, Bird – *On the Ground*

Doc Watson – *Cotton Eyed Joe, Shady Grove*

Gordon Lightfoot – *Pussywillows, Cat-Tails*

Harmonizing 4 – *Wade in the Water*

Israel Kamakawiwo'ole – *Over the Rainbow/ Wonderful World*

James Hill – *Down Rideau Canal*

Jerry Alfred & The Medicine Beat – *Salaw, The Grandfather Song/Etsi Shon*

John Lee Hooker – *It Serves You Right to Suffer*

Jorge Ben – *Errare Humanum Est*

Louis Armstrong – *La Vie en Rose*

Ludwig van Beethoven – *Symphony No. 6 in F Major, Op. 68 'Pastoral'*

Makaha Sons of Ni'ihau (with Israel Kamakawiwo'ole) – *Star of Gladness*

Manitoba Hal – *Line and Pole*

Miriam Makeba – *Pata Pata*

Mississippi Fred McDowell – *You Got to Move*

Nightingale – *Tickle Cove Pond/Over the Ice/ Culfadda*

Paul Winter – *Lay Down Your Burden, Common Ground, Ancient Voices (Nhmamusasa), Icarus*

Penguin Cafe Orchestra – *The Ecstasy of Dancing Fleas, Air a Danser*

Ralph Vaughan Williams – *The Lark Ascending, Romance for Violin and Orchestra*

Rory Block – *Walk in Jerusalem*

Sergio Mendes – *Waters of March*

Stéphane Grappelli & Django Reinhardt – *Swing 42*

Sue Smith – *I Need a Band and a Tango Partner*

Taj Mahal – *Freight Train*

The Isley Brothers – *Summer Breeze*

The Klezmatics with Joshua Nelson and Kathryn Farmer – *Elijah Rock*

The Lovin' Spoonful – *Do You Believe in Magic?*

The Rascals – *Groovin'*

Van Morrison – *Astral Weeks, Listen to the Lion* (live version from album *It's Too Late to Stop Now*)

Van Morrison & The Chieftains – *She Moved through the Fair*

Yungchen Lhamo – *Happiness Is...*

I would also highly recommend the two earliest Tamarack albums, *Music of Canada* and *A Pleasant Gale* (both with my brother, Jeff Bird), which have just become available online at http://www.latentrecordings.com/detail.php?al_id=52. If you can find the album *Rock The World* by the band Third World (I haven't been able to, but availability changes all the time), it's great too.

MUSIC-RELATED FILMS

Edward Gillan – *Desperate Man Blues*

Gregory Coyes – *How the Fiddle Flows*

Jean Doumanian and Barbara Kopple – *Wild Man Blues*

Les Blank – *J'ai Été au Bal/I went to the Dance; Puamana*

Martin Scorsese – *The Last Waltz*

Martin Scorsese – *The Blues*

Paul Balmer – *Stéphane Grappelli: A Life in the Jazz Century*

The Cowboy Junkies – *Long Journey Home*

The Mountain Apple Company – *IZ: The Man and His Music; Island Music, Island Hearts*

BOOKS

Beattie, Mac. *This Ottawa Valley of Mine*. Arnprior, Ont.: Beattie Music Inc., 1982.

Beloff, Jim. *The Ukulele: A Visual History (Revised & Expanded)*. San Francisco: Backbeat Books, 2003.

Campbell, Don. *The Mozart Effect: Tapping the Power or Music to Heal the Body, Strengthen the Mind and Unlock the Creative Spirit*. New York: Avon Books, 1997.

Cannel, Ward and Mrax, Fred. *How to Play the Piano Despite Years of Lessons: What Music Is and How to Make It at Home*. Paterson, NJ: Crown & Bridge Publishers, 1976.

Greene, Joshua M. *Here Comes The Sun: The Spiritual and Musical Journey of George Harrison*. Hoboken, NJ: John Wiley & Sons, 2006.

Handy, W.C. *Father of the Blues: An Autobiography*. New York: Collier, 1970 (first published 1941).

Hart, Mickey and Stevens, Jay. *Drumming at the Edge of Magic: A Journey into the Spirit of Percussion*. New York: HarperCollins, 1990.

Hodgkinson, Will. *Guitar Man: A Six-string Odyssey*. London: Bloomsbury Publishing, 2006.

Mahal, Taj and Foehr, Stephen. *Taj Mahal: Autobiography of a Bluesman*. London: Sanctuary, 2002.

Mezzrow, Mezz, and Wolfe, Bernard, *Really the Blues*. New York: Dell, 1946.

Reck, David. *Music of the Whole Earth*. New York: Charles Scribner's Sons, 1977.

Young, Peter. *Let's Dance: A Celebration of Ontario's Dance Halls and Summer Dance Pavilions*. Toronto: Natural Heritage/Natural History Inc., 2002.

If you want to continue this conversation with John Bird and other readers – and perhaps suggest some of your own favourite music – go to: http://spiritualityofmusic.blogspot.com

PHOTO AND ART CREDITS